THE TEACHING OF ECONOMICS IN
SECONDARY SCHOOLS

THE TEACHING OF
ECONOMICS IN
SECONDARY SCHOOLS

ASSISTANT MASTERS
ASSOCIATION

CAMBRIDGE
AT THE UNIVERSITY PRESS
1971

Published by the Syndics of the Cambridge University Press
Bentley House, 200 Euston Road, London N.W.1
American Branch: 32 East 57th Street, New York, N.Y. 10022

© Cambridge University Press 1971

ISBN: 0 521 08010 X

Printed in Great Britain
at the University Press
Aberdeen

CONTENTS

MEMBERS OF THE COMMITTEE

L. W. Dever (Chairman), *Xaverian College, Manchester*

F. W. G. Benemy (Vice-Chairman), *William Ellis School, London*

F. Brook (Secretary), *Staffordshire College of Technology, Stafford*

V. S. Anthony, *University of Leeds, Department of Education (formerly of Tonbridge School)*

D. P. Baron, *Xaverian College, Manchester*

J. C. Cox, *The Grammar School, Fleetwood*

C. J. Dakin, *Hele's School, Exeter*

D. Lee, *Rolle College, Exmouth (formerly of City of Bath School)*

G. Owen, *The Grammar School, Mexborough*

FOREWORD

There is no doubt that Economics is one of the growth points in the curriculum of secondary schools in England and Wales. The decision of the Association in 1966 to extend its series of books on the teaching of the main subjects in the secondary school curriculum was not taken lightly and has proved timely. The Association is indebted to the members of the Committee charged with the task of preparing this book, which is based very properly upon the knowledge and experience of classroom teachers of the subject.

The Committee acknowledges the assistance and encouragement it has received from members of the Association and would like to record its particular gratitude to those who were responsible for the final preparation of the manuscript.

I am confident that teachers of Economics in all types of secondary school will find much in this book which is of interest and help to them and that it will be of great value to teachers in training, to teachers in the early years of their careers and to teachers who have sole responsibility for teaching this subject in their school.

A. W. S. HUTCHINGS
July 1970   *Secretary, Assistant Masters Association*

INTRODUCTION

There are many books about Economics, but very few about how to teach Economics. As far as we know, there is, till now, no book which deals with teaching Economics solely in secondary schools. In writing the book we found ourselves in a quandary. Economics is still a growing subject and, at the present time, it is common for teachers to begin teaching Economics after years of experience in some other field. On the other hand there is an increasing flow of Economics graduates entering the teaching profession and beginning immediately to teach in their own specialist field. Thus, our object is to help both the young teacher to teach a subject with scarcely any traditional lore to support him and the experienced teacher who may be pioneering the organisation of a department.

This book is essentially a collective undertaking; the outcome of the experience of teaching in many different types of schools. Some members of the Committee have been teaching Economics for a long time; others are less experienced teachers but are more in touch with recent developments in Economics at university level. Most of the Committee are disciples of the 'new' Economics in which the mathematical approach predominates and where the atmosphere is one of devoted professionalism. Although we feel that our pooled ideas are better than the ideas of any individual Committee member, we do not think we have reached perfection. We do not intend to be dogmatic in any of our suggestions. If other teachers of Economics gain something from our ideas we shall be satisfied.

The teacher of today must be concerned with external examinations but we have interpreted our field as being wider than merely 'O' and 'A' level work in the secondary school because we feel that already Economics is becoming the core of a social science course in many schools and as such is being taught to many children who will never aspire to sixth-form work or to university. We would not like to think that the teacher is to become a slave to an examination syllabus. Rather we would prefer to see it used as a guide, and retain the traditional freedom of teaching which the British teacher enjoys. We welcome the work of the Schools Council in drawing the standards and syllabuses of the various examination boards closer

1

together and the tendency to give increasing scope to teachers to set and mark the examinations. The teacher should aim at developing in his pupils a reasonable knowledge of the subject gained from reading and writing about it, from taking part in lessons, from learning how to think in logical sequence and, in general, from developing an ability to learn at all levels.

A particular problem for the Economics teacher is that, although he may use an approach similar to that used in teaching the physical sciences, the unequivocal answers found to problems in those fields are not to be found to problems posed by the social sciences. It is desirable that pupils understand this characteristic of the social sciences rather than be given ready-made solutions which match one viewpoint only, tempting though this latter approach may be when faced with the rigours of external examinations. The enthusiasm of the teacher for his own subject and the methods of putting his material across to his pupils, allowing for age and ability differences, are aspects of teaching Economics which might well apply to teaching all other subjects, but which we feel it would be wrong to ignore.

One of the attractions of Economics is that it is a living subject and as such it is undergoing continuous development. New books are written, new methods of teaching are introduced and new ideas are put forward. It is an enormous task to keep abreast of these changes but the Economics teacher has to do it. It means the constant reading of new books, journals, periodicals and newspapers, watching television and listening to the radio. In order to keep up to date it is advisable to attend courses and conferences arranged by local authorities, by universities and by the Economics Association. It is extremely valuable to make contact with other teachers of Economics to discuss mutual problems and to interchange ideas.

The choice of textbooks can be a headache to all teachers because of the difficulty of finding books which suit the particular needs of teacher and class. In Economics teaching, because of the changing subject matter, textbooks soon become out of date and they must be kept constantly under review. We have tried to provide a wide book list mentioning books we have found to be useful and giving our reasons in the hope that it may serve as a guide to other teachers.

We have tried to look forward even if this means that some of our suggestions may appear to be impracticable and unrealistic at the moment. Reorganisation of the pattern of secondary education into comprehensive systems calls for the rethinking of many traditional ideas. We have tried to anticipate this and to make some suggestions about school syllabuses and teaching approaches.

1

THE ROLE OF ECONOMICS IN THE SECONDARY SCHOOL

Economics has several attractive characteristics: it is a live subject dealing with current and with future problems, it touches all our lives intimately, it is concerned with people, it studies one aspect of their behaviour and is therefore a very proper study at secondary school level.

One of the responsibilities of living in a democracy is to be informed about what is happening in society and to understand the issues involved. The world constantly changes and our lives with it. If we suspect that the 'good old days' never really existed we shall not be afraid to move forward with our society; to do so we must first strive to understand the nature of our ever more insistent present – and this partially but nonetheless importantly – through a study of those matters which are concerned with the economic behaviour of human beings.

The adolescent constantly strives to be accepted by the adult world and this involves him in an understanding of those aspects of human behaviour which may be defined as economic. Indeed, it is sometimes a lack of understanding of the economic issues that proves the teenager's stumbling block in his discussions with adults. A teenager does not become an adult overnight, nor can he learn to understand the adult system overnight. A study of Economics can help the student deal with these new problems. Here is a subject which helps him to see his role in society and the interdependence of all groups within that society. In his study of Economics he will become conscious of his own decisions, actions and responsibilities. In catering for the needs of those pupils who leave school at an early age Economics should be directly related to everyday life, avoiding a theoretical approach. The leaver will be interested in his weekly wage and the various deductions from it, in the various forms of saving open to him, in various types of banking accounts, in hire purchase and similar matters. In this way Economics could form part of a much wider course covering the various social services and institutions with which the new worker is likely to be concerned.

In reaction to the educational ideas of such thinkers as Rousseau, Tolstoy was perhaps the first to put into practical effect the idea of the importance to the child of the world outside school. In 1859 he defined education as 'a human activity' and established his village school at Yasnaya Polyana to educate the children of the serfs. In *The Aims of Education* (1929) A. N. Whitehead wrote, 'I would only remark that the understanding we want is an understanding of an insistent present'. John Dewey, echoing the motto of the London School of Economics, *Rerum Cognoscere Causas*, thought it essential to 'teach not so much things as the meaning of things'. We think that 'the world outside school', 'an insistent present', 'the meaning of things' are important facets of education which together form a positive assertion of the essential role that Economics has to play in the school curriculum. They are the matters with which Economics is concerned. Schools are beginning to recognise that we live in a world where a knowledge of Economics is of fundamental importance and on the strength of that recognition will depend the degree to which teachers of Economics consider themselves bound within the somewhat narrow limits of the demands of an examination syllabus. From the moment of birth to that of death our existence is influenced by the economic forces controlling the structure of our society. It is in this context that many schools introduce the subject into their timetables.

The need for an understanding of Economics

Professor J. K. Galbraith wrote: 'The first requirement for an understanding of contemporary economic and social life is a clear view of the relation between events and the ideas which interpret them. For each of these has a life of its own, and . . . each is capable for a considerable period of pursuing an independent course.' Often this relationship is obscure because the main criterion in the formulation of ideas interpreting events is their social acceptability. 'The ideas which are esteemed at any time for their acceptability' are what Professor Galbraith calls 'the conventional wisdom'. Part of the 'conventional wisdom' of the educational world is that the acceptable ideas are the familiar ideas and thus in education there is an inherent conservatism together with an endemic negativism where a triumph is merely a successful resistance to change. Educationists rarely pay much attention to economic criteria in the formulation and expression of their ideas. The administrators who write on the economics of education are rarely economists. It is hardly surprising that Economics has not enjoyed a more important role in the school curriculum when a large number of people charged with the promotion of educational ideas and their application to the practical problems of education consider that economic principles provide little that is useful in the solution of educational problems. It is encouraging that one of the new business schools is offering a course in management principles and practice for the headmasters of comprehensive schools. Under such stimuli as this it may become possible to consider the problems associated with the raising of the school leaving age, for instance, in terms of the opportunity costs to the community and the benefits that must accrue from the eventual more efficient use of better trained labour resources. In another context the raising of the school leaving age may be seen as an attempt to postpone unemployment. Only when educationists come to recognise the value to themselves of an understanding of economic ideas will there be the technical and social advance necessary not only in the field of education but in the community as a whole.

Economic understanding, which implies at least a basic knowledge of the operation of the economic system, is an essential part of everyone's education. If a child is to begin to understand the world in which he lives he must first understand some of the economic principles and institutions which determine its structure. Obviously not all schoolchildren are potential economists; yet they still need to understand the economic structure of the society of which they are already members. As students they are consumers faced with the basic problems of choice and the most efficient use of their resources. If they are to read newspapers meaningfully they must understand the economist's terms with some degree of precision; similarly in listening to the radio or watching television they are likely to hear such terms as 'trade gap' or 'demarcation dispute' which it is important that they should understand. Government economic policy has both a direct and an indirect influence on their lives both in the taxation changes that occur and in the degree to which the level of economic activity is determined through financial and fiscal controls. Students at school should have the opportunity to study these matters.

ROLE OF ECONOMICS IN THE SECONDARY SCHOOL

We think that the whole school benefits when Economics forms part of the timetable. All gain from the better informed discussions on current affairs, all benefit from the wider range of reading material which permeates into classrooms and libraries and all gain from outside speakers and industrial visits.

Economics in the school curriculum

In their other studies pupils will find a knowledge of basic economic ideas indispensable. There has been a tremendous growth in the study of Economic History in schools in recent years and, even though the barriers between the different branches of historical study are still rigidly maintained, it is tacitly realised by all teachers that the study of political events must make some reference to economic factors. Louis XIV owed his power and great international significance in the 1680s as much to economic as to military and political factors. Again, Geography is not merely a study of physical environment. Much of the importance of geographical study lies in what it has to tell us about the activities of man in his physical environment through emphasis on those branches of the study which are termed Economic and Human Geography. Whether you happen to be a geographical determinist, believing that physical environment determines the limit of man's activity, or not, geographical studies indicate the ways in which economic decisions and social policies have to be modified. In the same way that economists must be aware of geographical factors affecting their decisions, so geographers need a knowledge of economic principles if their statements are to be meaningful. Geologists and geographers may indicate the existence and stress the importance of the oil fields in the Exmouth Gulf region of Australia, but if the world price of oil is too low to make its extraction economically sound the oil will remain in the ground. Thus Economics, Geography and History are inextricably interrelated and a study of one must be accompanied by a knowledge of the others. Economics has been treated in the past as the Cinderella subject, but it may well be that, as our thirst for knowledge about our society and our behaviour continues to grow, we shall discover that the Social Sciences are the fountainhead of the other subjects. As a science concerned to explain one aspect of human behaviour, Economics leads on to the study of other

7

behavioural sciences such as Sociology, Psychology and Ethics. These studies are a natural development from basic economic ideas not merely in terms of their subject matter but also in the scientific methods employed in their investigations. Economics as a science is positive; it says what is rather than what ought to be. It is the study of these other behavioural sciences, particularly of Ethics, that can equip students to make normative judgments on economic behaviour.

The value of teaching Economics below the sixth form

In many schools Economics is taught only at sixth form level. Arguments have been advanced, from time to time, in favour of teaching Economics to children of all ages including those in primary schools. Leaving aside the question of primary education, there is a strong case for the inclusion of the subject as an integral course of study in the curriculum for pupils of fourteen to sixteen years of age in all types of secondary school. It is important that the pupil leaving school at sixteen is prepared in every way for the world in which he will live, work and take his leisure. If his activities are to be well-ordered and if he is to enjoy and to fulfil his role as a citizen effectively, the inevitable upheaval, caused by his quitting the closed and protected environment of school and home, must be cushioned by carefully introducing him to the world he will meet when school days are over. In this sphere of education a study of economic affairs has a major role to play. Thus in the discussions on curricula developments consequent upon the publication of 'Half Our Future', the Newsom Report, and the decision to raise the school leaving age, the importance of the need to teach the pupil about his society and environment must emerge. By studying the structure of various industries and by discussing their problems the student's experience is expanded. Through works visits the child is taken out of the class-room and made aware of an entirely new world with new possibilities and difficulties. By seeing a wide range of industries and through individual research the child is indirectly forming impressions that will help him make a more rational choice of career. The student realises that many of the topics with which he is dealing will be of direct benefit to him when he leaves school: an understanding of taxation, national insurance, even the role of trade unions will help him to adapt himself to the adult world more easily.

Economics in the sixth form

An understanding of Economics is important if a sixth-form student is to begin to understand his environment and the many facets of human behaviour and if he is to take an intelligent and responsible part in the life of the community. It is in this sphere that we begin to see C. P. Snow's suggestion that the social sciences may be 'the bridge between the two cultures' – arts and sciences – being put into practical effect. Increasingly, Economics is taken in combination with both science and arts subjects, as in the combination History, Mathematics with Statistics and Economics at Advanced level. Although not all sixth-form Economics students entering universities will intend reading Economics for their degree, it may well be that many will find that they are required to read the subject as part of a much wider course of study as in Sociology, Politics, Statistics or Engineering. It is, however, extremely important that students not taking Economics to Advanced level should be given the opportunity to study the subject in minority time as part of their general education. It is here that the science student can gain a better appreciation of the implications of his special interests, can gain some idea of the sources of industrial investment, the structure of industry and the implications for his work of various aspects of governmental policy decisions. Such an appreciation can only serve to make his approach to his studies more realistic. Here the arts student can see the workings of government and the contrasts between developed and under-developed nations or even begin to understand the point of many of the Prefaces to the plays of George Bernard Shaw.

Economics as a major subject in the sixth form

There is no doubt that when the subject is studied systematically to a higher level it does help to produce an approach to school work which is both logical and objective. By learning to reject purely emotional or biased argument, by learning to interpret and use a wide range of statistical material the student is trained to present a carefully reasoned argument. He also learns to question until he is satisfied, to criticise but to be constructive in his criticism.

In these ways Economics aims to train the mind as well as to impart information. Economics must explain with a high degree of accuracy and acceptability the complexities of that part of human and political behaviour which is concerned with the way in which the community conducts its business affairs. If the student is to equip himself to deal with these complexities well, he must be trained to handle and to think in terms of the effects of many variable factors simultaneously and so to understand clearly the relationships between the factors themselves; this is the essence of economic insight. Teachers employ the methods of designing and building theoretical models of economic behaviour and modifying the assumptions on which these models are based in the light of their application to real world situations. Once we begin to apply the idea of perfect competition to market activities in the real world we quickly have to modify our assumptions about freedom to enter the market, about homogeneity of products, about the effects of differences in the quantity and quality of the labour supply. We discover very quickly that the *ceteris* are far from being *paribus* and so, to the student, the model of the firm's behaviour in a perfectly competitive market becomes a concept which influences his pattern of thinking rather than a piece of information to be learned by rote and re-gurgitated in some future examination. The exercise of applying the model to actual business situations conditions the student to dealing with the effects of many variable factors; for instance, to explain the decisions of firms in an oligopolistic market in terms of the security of their relative market positions and security of profits rather than in terms of optimum outputs and profit maximisation; in terms of full cost pricing principles rather than marginal cost pricing rules. The student is now in a position to understand the complex arguments surrounding the abolition of resale price maintenance, to understand some of the more common fallacies inherent in the idea of 'competition' and to work out for himself that, under an oligopolistic market structure, non-price competition may, in the long run, be more advantageous to consumer interests than price competition. The inculcation of that attitude of mind in the student where he becomes aware of the numerous forces which have to be taken into account to arrive at a valid analysis of a situation – the starting point from which a policy decision is made – holds the widest of educational implications for the teaching of Economics in schools. Such training can be and is being carried out, albeit at the moment in a small way, in sixth-form studies. University teachers may well discredit the idea that a seventeen-year-old can discover for himself the relative merits and demerits of resale price maintenance, but the argument is not so difficult to understand if the student's attitude of mind has been carefully developed. In other disciplines such as Algebra we demand a great deal more in terms of abstract reasoning from fourteen-year-olds than we demand of students of Economics whose capabilities are frequently underestimated. The paramount task of a teacher of Economics thus becomes the inculcation of the understanding of an insistent present. We must believe with J. M. Keynes that 'Economics is a method rather than a doctrine, an apparatus of the mind, a technique of thinking'.

If the student develops in his Economic studies the versatility of thinking which it is the aim of his teacher to inculcate in him, he will find an exploration of Economics not only greatly enlightening, but immensely exciting. The teacher of Economics has a great initial advantage: the student is on his side. The teacher is talking about the student's life, environment and society. To learn to look at familiar things in a new way, to feel the development of his mind and the broadening of his understanding and vision taking place, can be and ought to be for the student a thrilling experience. Thus a major role of Economics in the sixth form is to provide an atmosphere in which the student can explore and develop the potentialities of his intellect in a tremendously stimulating, yet soundly logical and scientific pattern. The popular misunderstanding of Carlyle's reference to 'the dismal science' is no longer applicable.

The growth of Economics as a school subject

Today Economics is being taught in a rapidly increasing number of schools. At one time teachers of the subject in universities discouraged the idea that it was a suitable subject for students at school. This scepticism was perhaps the product of two factors: that sixth formers who took Economics were the least able students in the school, and that teachers were not professional economists. Neither of these things is true today.

2

ECONOMICS AS A SOCIAL STUDY
FOR ALL CHILDREN

The Aim

We are concerned, not only with the academically able children, who will eventually take Advanced level, but with all children. Every child should leave school with some knowledge of the economic and political society in which he, or she, is about to work and earn a living, probably marry and bring up a family. Present trends suggest that in the near future there will be a social studies course for pupils from the age of eleven which will help to make all school-leavers good citizens. School-leavers will know that they cannot take anything out of the common store of wealth unless they put something into it, that the more they contribute, the richer will be the community. We want them to understand the role of man in society and the real nature of the Welfare State.

The family as the unit of society

At the age of twelve, the child has had little experience of life. His main social experiences have been gained with the family of which he is part and with the group with whom he works and plays, in and out of school. Therefore we begin with the structure of the family. Explain that we are a monogamous society and that the family consists of a father and a mother, and the pupil's brothers and sisters, not to mention his grand-parents, his uncles and aunts, and his cousins. The family live in a house or flat. Already the child will probably have experienced both harmony and happiness at home, and conflict and strain as well. Why does he live in a council flat instead of a detached house with a big garden? Why does his mother work hard cooking and dusting, making the beds and darning socks, going out shopping and being at home to give him tea when he gets home from school? Why does she scold him when he gets his blazer dirty or his feet wet? Why does his father grumble when the child is noisy and restless at home and does not want to do his homework? You can explain that the role of the adults is to give children the benefit of their experience and wisdom; you can point out that the class has the opportunity in school to train for an adult role by taking responsibility as prefects and leaders of younger children. You can remind them of other people who are handicapped by old age, sickness, deafness or blindness, who need help. You can show them how we all depend on each other, and why they should be willing to help others. You can point out how this mutual interdependence of people has resulted in a society of specialists, why the division of labour will be beneficial only if we co-operate with each other and exchange the surpluses we produce.

Wealth and its distribution

Some people are rich and others are poor. How is a household budget calculated? What does the average family earn in a week? How does the family spend this money? What do they consume? How much do they save? How do they save; by having an insurance policy or buying stamps or premium bonds or opening a savings bank account at the post office or even keeping a piggy bank at home? Why do we save? Is it not more enjoyable to spend all our money now while we are young? Do we borrow money? Is buying a house with a mortgage or a car with a hire purchase agreement borrowing? Is borrowing socially good or bad? Is it better to save and wait until we have enough money to buy a television set which shows colour programmes or do we rent such a set? Why do people lend money? Is charging interest a bad thing? Is it greedy? When we look for a job, do we take the one that pays the most money now or do we choose one that offers the prospects of high income in the future? Is the pay the only reward we think about when we take a job, or are there other things equally important? Why does a girl decide to become a nurse, or a boy a priest when neither of these occupations pays such good wages as being a film star or a professional footballer? Discuss these things, encourage the children to talk, to express their opinions, and to make value-judgments.

The needs of man

Talk about man's needs. Discuss the importance of food and shelter and clothing. How would they like a perennial diet of bread and

13

ECONOMICS FOR ALL CHILDREN

cheese, water or milk, apples or pears? They would soon tire of such a monotonous diet. Where do the oranges and lemons come from or the tea and coffee, or the chocolate? Trace the chain of production from the planting of wheat seed, perhaps in Canada, to the baking of a loaf of bread in an English town.

Why do children go to school?

Talk about the importance of education. We all have an equal opportunity in the Welfare State to learn how to make a living when we leave school. If we know how to learn, we can be taught relatively easily to work a computer or a typewriter, to find out what is wrong with the car when it breaks down, to build a house or plough a field and do all the apparently complicated jobs that need to be done. You can explain to your pupils the importance of technology, the trains and tubes, the telephone and the telegraph, the radio and television, the ship and the jet aeroplane, which have transformed our lives, brought us all nearer to each other; you can point out the economic consequences of the enormous improvements in transport and communications which enable us to have bananas for breakfast or New Zealand butter for tea, brought to us in the ships equipped with refrigerators. You don't have to draw elaborate mathematical models on the blackboard in order to teach children Applied Economics.

Value-judgments

They are not too young to start making value-judgments. Why does Thomasinia Chimbligg like apple dumplings better than ice cream, while Mary Ramsbottom prefers Brussels sprouts to artichokes? What is Willie Wintergreen going to do when he gets home tonight? Will he watch the Western on B.B.C. or I.T.V.? He can't watch both because they are on simultaneously. Persuade him to think why he prefers the 'Lone Ranger' to 'The Virginian'. Why did the Westminster Bank amalgamate with the National Provincial Bank? You can go on almost endlessly; encourage the class to think of dilemmas which confront them and explain why they chose to do this rather than that, why they often regret the decision and wish they had done something else. They are learning the essence of Economics in a practical way.

14

Personal experience

At the age of twelve or thirteen, the child, however intelligent, has little experience of life, and has never thought about social problems. You have the difficult task of generating a desire to think about economic matters as an essential part of everyone's life, of creating a motivation to learn. The child already has an enquiring mind and an impressionable memory; you have to persuade him or her to steer some of the enquiries into the direction of economic affairs. This you can best do by awakening an interest in them in real things, rather than abstract theories that need adult perceptiveness; common or garden everyday affairs that are the business of us all. At this stage, when there is no examination to worry about, you will probably find a sociological approach best. Persuade the class to observe what is going on around them and to enquire whether these happenings have anything to do with them. Make use of their experience from day to day. You are making the class conscious of certain facts which have economic significance and which have a personal connection with them. You will find that as the children grow older and their work in class becomes more advanced the structure will develop. The association of ideas will stimulate them to making discoveries for themselves. We believe firmly in the idea of structure building, from one age group to the next, in exploiting the growing, widening experiences of the children, in gradually connecting facts with basic economic concepts, in paving the way for the introduction of some theory and analysis.

Poverty and wealth

Talk about poverty and wealth. What is poverty? What is wealth? Is poverty relative or absolute? Is an English family living in a small council flat, with an income of £15 a week richer or poorer than an Indian peasant tilling his own small piece of land living on what he grows? Is Mr Jones richer than an Eskimo because he has a refrigerator and the Eskimo hasn't? Is Mr Smith wealthier than Mr Olusanya, the Nigerian, because Mr Smith has central heating and Mr Olusanya hasn't? Some people have the bathroom and the lavatory in one room, others have them separate, a few have two bathrooms and two cloakrooms. Why is this? Are the poorer people envious and resentful? If so, what do they do about this disparity?

15

Do they break in and steal from their more affluent neighbours or burn their houses down or do they work harder to get more money or do they combine to form a pressure group and elect a member to parliament and have progressive taxes passed by parliament to redistribute income? You can personalise these economic problems. You can even dramatise them. You can certainly get the children to think about affairs which are part and parcel of their daily lives. You can explain the role of the Welfare Society in all this.

The aims of taxation

We all pay at least one 'tax' if we work, national insurance, for which we get free medical attention, an allowance when we are out of a job and a pension when we are too old to work. Those of us who earn enough pay income tax and some of us pay surtax. This money is spent on providing free education, on subsidising school meals, on providing a police force, paying and equipping soldiers, sailors and airmen, and so on. Those who own or rent houses pay rates, which are spent by local government councils on clearing the dustbins and cleaning and lighting the streets, and on schools and police. There is usually something which the council is doing that you can talk about, like building a housing estate, returfing the tennis courts on the common or putting up a pavilion in the park where refreshments can be purchased. You can bring out the fact that your pupils are members of a community and that these amenities are provided for the community. Try to make the children think of emergencies in which they find the telephone of vital importance; there has been an accident, someone has been hurt, you want the police and the ambulance to come along at once, so you make an emergency call. There would be a serious delay if telephone kiosks were few and far between. We are humanitarian civilised people who do not want anyone in pain, and we also want our labour force to be as strong and healthy as possible. We don't realise how important the posting and delivering of letters is until our mail is held up. You can go on from Christmas cards and birthday cards to business letters, ordering goods, paying bills, writing to a firm a long way off. A businessman in your town is anxious to get in touch with a merchant in Hong Kong. He can reach him in four days by air mail or phone him in a few minutes. The local shoemaker does not make shoes any more.

He doesn't have to because he can order the shoes he sells from a factory in Northampton and get them delivered to him in a few days. Many of the children come to school by bus. They have free passes for the bus. They have to queue up for the buses. They know what happens when the bus is late. They are late for school. The teachers are angry. They miss a lesson or part of a lesson. The same sort of thing is true of business people. If they are late for work, trade is lost. They may even forfeit some wages. If they are late home from work, the meal is cold when they are hungry and tired. Our output of goods and services will dwindle if we do not all do our share. We are all dependent on each other.

You can point out that the pillar boxes, the telephone kiosks, the buses are all for the benefit of the community. Ask your pupils to go out and plot the sites and numbers of these material proofs of the helping hand of the Welfare State. Remind them that these services are not gifts of providence, that the community has to work hard to provide them.

Living in groups

You have been talking quite a lot about the community. You should now discuss the problems of living in the country in a small village or living in a big town, as most of the children probably do. Why are the streets so crowded with people and traffic? Why do people like to live in cities? Do they consider the cinemas and dance halls, the theatres and ballets and concerts, the libraries and museums, the football clubs and shops a great advantage? Why do people queue patiently to buy a ticket to watch Manchester United play Tottenham Hotspur? Why are there more applicants for seats to watch Margot Fonteyn dance than there are seats? Why are seats more expensive in city cinemas than in suburban ones? Why do we, living on the outskirts of the town, have to wait before Julie Andrews' latest film comes to the local cinema? Why, when there are so many people milling round, can one person feel lonely and unhappy? Here is your chance to talk about mass production in big factories. The employers or entrepreneurs need workers and the employees or wage-earners need jobs. So both come to live in the city. Here is a market both for goods and for labour. Here is a variety of jobs to choose from, a bewildering diversity of goods to buy. You cannot

17

possess them all partly because you do not have enough money and partly because you could not consume them or store them, so you make a choice. Why does the fishmonger sell fruit and chickens, while the newsagent sells sweets as well as tobacco? How many departments are there in the big store in the High Street? Why do Marks and Spencer display their goods so that the customer can see exactly what the shop has to sell, what the price is, what the size of the shirt is, whether it is made of cotton or nylon? Why do Boots sell cosmetics and perfumes as well as medicines? How do people use their leisure?

Working for a living

You can now talk about hours of work, about employers and workers. Why does the bank open to the public at 10 a.m. and shut at 3 p.m.? Why is Wednesday early closing day for the shops? Why are trade unions often arguing about working hours? Why does all work and no play make Jack a dull boy while all play and no work makes Jill a dull girl? We have a break at school, the children rush out into the playground, the noise is deafening; have they noticed any more willingness to tackle the next lesson after the break? Why do we have holidays? And why do we have homework? Why do we have school rules? Why do we have detentions and lines? Why don't we beat children like we used to do? There are parallels between an adult's working life and a child's school life. They have more experience of what it is like to work for a living than they realise until these parallels are explored.

The idea of discipline

Now we are ready to talk about crime and punishment, rights and duties, law and order. You can no doubt find many opportunities to show how an absence of law and order in school may make life exciting and enjoyable for a time, but the chaos and damage would in the end ruin the school. You can point out that we tend to take things for granted. We assume that the bus will bring us to school, that the school timetable works out to plan, the teachers and the class both turn up in the right room for a lesson, the blackboard is clean, there is chalk and a duster, there are ample desks to sit at, the lights go on, there are books and maps; someone has made arrangements that work smoothly. Our time is not wasted. The training and skill of the teacher are being usefully employed. The children's parents are happy to accumulate valuable pieces of furniture at home because they are reasonably sure that their property is going to be safe. You can combine explaining the relationship between crime and punishment in real life, in school and in economic affairs. You can talk about our rights and duties as citizens. We have inspectors of weights and measures to make sure that shopkeepers do not cheat us; we have company law that lays down that the accounts of a firm must be audited; we have a Consumer's Council; we have a Monopolies Commission and a Restrictive Practices Court. We can work where we like in our own country; we can say what we like so long as we don't infringe the laws of libel or slander. We will get the vote when we are eighteen. We cannot be arrested and held in custody unless a charge is made against us. You can point out the desirability of working and earning a living, of insuring against accidents, of putting aside money for a pension, of co-operating with other people. You can explain how in the Welfare State we aim at full employment, that we think we owe it to the dignity of a man to find him a job with a decent wage so that he does not have to depend on charity, that we induce him to join in a national insurance plan and when he retires at 65 he will get a pension. At this stage the children will begin to realise that a society is a complex organism with many problems outside the realm of the purely economic. That the economic, sociological and ethical problems of society are all interrelated and therein lies the complexity of a society.

Groups within society

As the children grow older and are able to make sounder value-judgments you can start to discuss pressure groups, trade unions, employers and employees, social classes, mobility from class to class or from job to job, hours of work, race, enquiries and polls. If this kind of work is successful, perhaps you might introduce a study of some other country, probably an underdeveloped one, in Asia or Africa; you can make some interesting comparisons. There are probably several spectacular events, which they read about or see on television, like a march to No. 10 Downing Street to present

19

a petition to the Prime Minister, which from time to time you can discuss with them. Perhaps you could found a class trade union to protect the interest of school children, hold meetings and talk about school hours, the break and homework, the school dinners or uniform. You can illustrate the benefits of patient negotiation and explain to them how collective bargaining has become the normal way of fixing wages today. They will understand why, when they leave school, they will be paid the rate for the job. Every now and then a trade union or professional association in real life will be having a dispute on wages that becomes a major news item and the class can take an interested part in this by following the negotiations, and listening to the arguments of both sides. You can bring out here the importance of consultation, that the unions like to be treated as responsible people, who think about their work, who might have fruitful ideas on methods of working and who resent being ignored.

Consumers and producers

You can use lessons about people to teach the theory of population. Discuss social class. What is the middle class? Do we place someone in the middle class because he went to a public school, or has an educated voice, or follows a learned profession or earns relatively large pay, or lives in a detached house in a quiet, respectable street? Who are the working class today when we all work? Is the Victorian idea of one's station in life gone for ever, or do we have ambitions to climb the social ladder or do we believe in an egalitarian society? It might be worth keeping a record of school teams and watch their progress through life. Where do they go to work? Do they stay in the home town or venture far afield? You could combine this part of your syllabus of work with an environmental study. Get hold of a classified telephone directory of the district and work out the number of different occupations listed and the number of people among the professions and the trades such as doctors and solicitors, estate agents and accountants, plumbers and carpenters, builders and electricians; how many banks are there in the town, how many schools, how many police stations? The class will get a very clear picture of the way in which the town earns its living. Make a list of the factories by type of goods produced and find out if the district concentrates on producing one type only or varies its output between washing machines and record-players, sparking plugs and electric kettles, and so on. Write to the managers of the factories and ask them to supply information about output and number of people employed. They will usually help.

You can ask each boy or girl in the school how many brothers and sisters he or she has. If they have neighbours whose children do not come to the school how many children are there in the family? What are the ages of all their children? You can produce a small census. You can keep a record from the local press of the ages of the people whose deaths are reported until you have some idea of the expectation of life.

You can explain why people live longer today than in 1900. They are better fed and housed. Their bodies are not worn out by long hours of exhausting physical toil. They are able to enjoy more leisure like holidays with pay and relax in front of the television. You can go on to talk about the standard of living and the cost of living. Put up an example of a family budget on the blackboard and ask each member of the class to produce a personal budget. If Myrtle Murgatroyd were married and had four children to bring up and her husband was a bus driver earning £25 a week, how would she spend her money? If Bill Brownbread was a doctor earning £3,750 a year and had two children, how would he spend his money? If Harold Hardcastle was the local M.P. with a family of four, how would he lay out his income? Have discussion on the sort of budgets you get. Make out a list of things that you think are essential if a family is to enjoy the good life. Find out how far the class agree with you. If the parents do not mind joining in the game, let them advise the children. When you have put together a representative list of essential things let the children go out and find out how much each of these items cost. You draw them into the lesson, make them do most of the work, induce them to think, and teach them Economics at the same time. This may not be academic, but you are laying firm foundations, and you never can tell where the enquiry will end.

Family and individual budgets

A sample budget taken from a national newspaper shows: gross wage of a man with a wife and two small children is £25 per week; net wage (after payment of tax, superannuation, etc.) is £20·31 per week.

Expenditure (per week) is:

	£
Mortgage	4·35
Rates	1·21
Solid fuel	1·30
Clothes	0·75
Food	8·50
Holidays	1·00
Car insurance and tax	0·45
Petrol	0·75
T.V. licence	0·10
Wife's pocket money	0·50
School meals	0·25
Personal pocket money	1·15
Total	**20·31**

Another example is of a professional man with a wife and three children (two at boarding school) with a gross income of £3,750 per annum.

Expenditure (per annum) is:

	£
Taxes	360
Rates	140
Superannuation	240
Insurance (life, etc.)	240
Mortgage	240
Fuel (electricity and gas)	150
Car hire purchase agreement and tax, licence, petrol	250
Wife's pocket money	260
Personal pocket money	260
Two children's boarding school fees	800
Food	500
Holidays	200
Clothes	100
Unaccounted for	10
Total	**3,750**

You could provoke an argument about the school fees. Why spend money on an expensive boarding school when there is a 'free' grammar school which gives as good an education? Is liberty to spend your money in your own way important? You could have an interesting discussion on why superannuation, life insurance, and a mortgage are regarded as socially desirable by the government, who allow tax concessions on income spent on these payments.

Another sample budget could be that of a teenager who left school at fifteen plus, is now eighteen plus, has a job and earns £14 per week gross and £12 net. How does he spend his money?

	£
Contribution to family exchequer	1·50
Motor-cycle, petrol, etc.	1·50
Fares, lunches, etc.	0·50
Clothes	2·00
Payments on records, record-player,	
transistor radio, etc.	1·50
Holidays	1·00
Girl-friend	1·50
Personal pocket money – on football,	
drinks, sweets, etc.	1·50
Insurance, saving stamps, etc.	1·00
Total	12·00

Have his parents the right to ask for a contribution to house-keeping? Is he foolish to offer one? Does he spend too much on consumer goods that give only immediate passing satisfaction? Is he needlessly prudent at so tender an age to use £1 per week on insurance or savings? There could be a lively discussion on these matters.

The class as a firm

You could assemble a board to consider a disputed wage claim. You could be the chairman who is to arbitrate, but better still allocate it to a pupil. Choose your trade union and employers' representatives, let them submit arguments in favour of a standard of living and offer budgets to prove the cost of living. Make sure they try to identify a rise in wages with productivity. There is no bottomless purse from which higher wages can flow endlessly. More pay and greater productivity must go together, otherwise there will be inflation. Next time you have a formal lesson you can talk about inflation, describe its principal characteristics, mention the chief causes. With a class of this kind you cannot attempt an ambitious academic enquiry into inflation, but you can work out a compre-hensible picture of it, you can most certainly point out its evils if it

23

is unchecked, you can explain why workers are sometimes asked by a government to act with restraint.

You can borrow a film about the Stock Exchange and if you live in London you can visit the Exchange, see the film there and also have a guide talk about the business on the floor. The film brings out the motto of the Stock Exchange 'My Word is my Bond' which is related to your theme. You can start up a joint-stock company, a private one, connected with a family, one of the children can be a member of the family and the chairman of the firm; play a drama of transforming a partnership into a joint-stock company; go to a merchant bank and borrow money. In due course your company grows into a public one and you can apply to the Stock Exchange Council for permission to be listed there. You will by now have decided what you are going to produce. You can choose a board of directors and hold a meeting at regular intervals to consider supply and demand, changes in price, distribution of dividends, relations with the staff through a meeting at which wages, hours and welfare will come up. Approach some big firms who will be pleased to send you copies of their annual reports and accounts.

The idea of a school firm offers almost endless possibilities and we hope that we have given you some ideas on which you can work. This method of teaching and learning is a fascinating project, which has in it something of the approach of the Nuffield scheme, since you are taking pupils who are practical people rather than academic and letting them learn by doing things, rather than read about them. This need not mean that they will do no reading: on the contrary, we are confident that the fieldwork will stimulate the desire to read and to record what has been done.

This kind of classwork must, of course, be varied regularly by more formal lessons in which you discuss what has been done, sum it up, point out the economic lessons that have been learned, the theories that have emerged, write out on the blackboard definitions of the concepts, tendencies, predictions and the laws of Economics, so that your pupils have some conventional knowledge as well as a lot of practical wisdom and know-how. Some testing may be needed to check what has been learned. To minimise the time spent on this, it can be done by short objective-type questions. We shall be surprised if you do not succeed in producing some economists with ambitions to pursue the discipline further.

TEACHING OF ECONOMICS IN SECONDARY SCHOOLS

A suggested syllabus for 4 years

YEAR 1. AN INTRODUCTORY, OR PRIMARY COURSE

The family as a work group.

Choice – relation between wants and resources; relative scarcity (the cricket bat or tennis racquet but not both).

Division of labour – the bread winner; the responsibility of earning a living (Dad is a policeman and not a ballet dancer) or (Dad in the office or factory; Mum as the centre of the family in providing personal services).

The need to work to produce in order to satisfy current wants.

Exchange – the process of satisfying those wants.

Occupations and income differences.

Inter-family comparison – in time, in place, wealth.

Saving for future consumption – saving for a purpose (the family car wears out, saving up for a cycle).

YEARS 2 AND 3. SUB-SYSTEMS OF SOCIETY

(*Note:* It is difficult to distinguish between year 2 and year 3; it is wiser to let the teacher decide for himself.)

The firm – a simple introduction to the co-operation between producers to produce a variety of complicated goods.

The factors of production.

Types of firms – the sole trader, the private company, the public company, the co-operative, public enterprise.

Markets – The profit motive, supply, demand and price.

Size of firms.

Organisation of firms.

Historical and geographical comparisons.

Limitations to specialisation and scales of production. For example, a town of 10,000 will not have a heart specialist or a university.

Efficiency

Institutions – Functions of money; financial enterprises (saving banks, commercial banks, hire purchase firms, stock exchanges, a discount market).

Trade unions – employers and professional associations – their functions.

Industrial disputes and their settlement.

Determination of wages.

YEAR 4. THE STATE AND SOCIETY: A NATIONAL VIEW

The role of Government in the economy.

Provision of goods and services to satisfy collective wants.

Government control of factors of production.

Government policy (taxation, full employment, stability of prices, control of wages, balance of payments).

Redistribution of income through social services.

Control of labour from other countries (immigration policy).

Spending of money at home and abroad.

Distribution of labour force.

Wealth – standard of living.

Income – cost of living.

Fluctuations in prosperity – the trade cycle.

Economic growth – investment.

END OF YEAR 4, OR START OF YEAR 5

Economics is one of several social sciences each connected with the others.

B   25

The comparative study of population in six different studies (or disciplines)

This will apply either (a) to a general social sciences course, or (b) to six different subjects, or (c) as a basis for History and Geography treated in a broad and liberal sense. (This table does not pretend to cover all possible aspects; it is mainly intended to be a guide, a basis for the thinking of the teacher.)

History	Geography	Economics	Politics	Sociology	Demography
Facts and figures of growth	Forms and growth of settlement	Size of population and distribution by: age, sex, location, industry	Size, growth and distribution for voting purposes	Effects of growth especially in cities and the sort of society that evolves	Birth and death rates
The emancipation of women	Influence of transport and communication	Future growth and its effect on division of labour	Urban and rural settlements for purposes of constituencies	Process of social differentiation	Fertility rates
The spread of education	Effect of climate on division of labour	The influence of an ageing population	Division into parties on economic and other grounds in a state like Cyprus	Immobility of labour created by social habits and customs, racial and religious differences, prejudices	Fashion of big families or small ones
The influence of the Industrial Revolution on migration from country to town	Influence on population of natural physical barriers	Mobility and its influence over employment		Family size	Early marriages
The influence of migration (say) from Europe to U.S.A., Australia and other new countries	Mining and manufacturing and the location of industry	The family as a source of demand and labour			Predictions as to rates of growth

3

ECONOMICS BELOW THE SIXTH FORM

Although Economics is still predominantly a sixth-form subject, increasingly the subject is included, in one form or another, in the lower and middle school curriculum. In chapter 2 we discussed how Economics could become a part of the education of all children of secondary school age, the emphasis being placed on a more informal social studies course with a strong vocational content. In this chapter we are concerned to outline a more formal, somewhat more academic, less vocational and certainly less wide-ranging course at the end of which the pupil would be fitted to sit a public examination for either the Certificate of Secondary Education or the Ordinary level of the General Certificate of Education. Such a course may last for five or two years; at the end of it the pupil may take Economics for C.S.E. or G.C.E., or he may sit for one of the newer combined subjects such as the Joint Matriculation Board's Economic and Public Affairs. There are many variations on this theme, so that we have divided the chapter into two parts; the first dealing with the teaching of the subject below the fifth form where the demands of any future public examination will be neither so pressing nor so apparent. The second part deals with the teaching of Economics in the fifth form, where the decision about whether the pupil is to sit for the C.S.E. or G.C.E. or not will have been taken and where the teaching method will vary accordingly.

A. ECONOMICS BELOW THE FIFTH FORM

Because Economics has been traditionally a sixth-form subject, the Economics teacher must be particularly careful to adapt his approach to classes below the sixth form. The variety and challenge of teaching a subject at different levels in the school can be a great gain to the teacher. We recommend that heads of Economics departments should, where possible, teach at all levels where Economics is studied in their schools.

The pattern of Economics lessons

The teacher should be clear in his own mind about what he intends to do with his class. He may be given a syllabus for the year to teach to, or he may have to prepare one for himself. In either case this does not help much with individual lessons. It is very unlikely, and very undesirable, that a teacher in September would be able to say 'On the third Tuesday in March, I will be dealing with the location of industry with the fourth form'. The treatment of a syllabus should be flexible to allow for taking up points as they develop naturally from the class, particularly in Economics where topical events have a bearing on particular parts of the course. Whilst avoiding extreme rigidity which may often produce a dull stereotyped approach, the teacher should be aware of the confusion that an approach which is over-flexible can produce. For most teachers their approach is determined through experience, in knowing whether a lesson has been side-tracked by a fascinating but time-wasting red herring, or whether a worthwhile topic has been discussed, out of turn but better for being of interest to the class at a particular time.

It is helpful to a teacher if he decides initially which teaching techniques he intends to use with each class and plans his general pattern of lessons. For instance, with a fourth-year class preparing for an examination at the end of the fifth year, and having four teaching periods per week and one homework period per week, the pattern might be: one period to introduce a new topic; one period leading up to the homework indicating clearly the treatment expected; one 'spare' period, and one period discussing the homework and showing clearly what went wrong for some boys and why some were better than others. The 'spare' period is an opportunity to try out some of the many suggestions offered later in this book – an occasional film, a tape recording, role-playing or perhaps a visiting speaker. We do not suggest that you become a variety performer, offering one of these 'novelties' every week. Two or three a term are probably sufficient. In most weeks this period could be used to check on notebooks, add to newspaper files or discuss current affairs which have an economic explanation or content.

Elsewhere, the question of note-taking is dealt with in some detail. We are by no means unanimous in our views on this matter but on balance we feel that the ideal, even for beginners at this stage, is for them to make their own notes, having been given guidance on the main points to look for. We realise that in fact, especially with a wide ability range, many children fall short of the ideal, hence the need to inspect notebooks regularly and the need to supplement occasionally with brief dictated or duplicated notes on specific topics.

Likewise, various ideas for building up newspaper files are dealt with later, but it is perhaps worthwhile to say something here with particular reference to young pupils at the stage we are considering. It is usually easy to get them to collect cuttings. Initially, of course, they tend to be very unselective and to go for quantity rather than for relevance. Nevertheless time spent in showing why one pupil's small item is more useful than another pupil's mountain of articles, is worthwhile. Above all, if the habits of newspaper reading and collecting cuttings are encouraged, they go a long way to broadening the scope of the subject and making pupils realise that they are dealing with a living subject which is not confined to the pages of a textbook or within the classroom walls.

Teaching techniques

A general pattern, such as this, still leaves wide scope for the teacher to choose the way in which he presents topics. If you are inexperienced you may feel inclined to lean heavily on the textbook, on the grounds that here is an experienced writer using a well tried and proven approach. Much depends on the class – some weak pupils will find most textbooks too difficult to absorb easily, other abler ones will find textbooks inadequate in their treatment of most topics. Generally, children up to fourteen or so, those who would come into this 'beginner' group, like the assurance of a textbook, feeling secure with the authority of the printed word. By all means point out the limitations of textbooks to them when necessary, but we feel that the deliberate denigration of textbooks with the intention of encouraging independent judgment is more suited to sixth-form work and when done at too early a stage can lead to confusion in the minds of the pupils.

The form of the lesson is again a matter for individual taste and judgment. Discussions are favoured by many teachers but leave several pitfalls to be avoided. It is easy for the discussion to become a monologue by the teacher, and few teachers are able to keep the interest of a class for half an hour of solid talking. Likewise two or three talkers within the class can dominate the discussion leaving the teacher with the impression of a lively and successful lesson, whereas many of the class have been completely disinterested or some may feel frustrated at not having had a chance to voice their views. Debates are often popular with the class and as an occasional event the formal debating approach can be stimulating, but to be worthwhile all the participants must prepare their contributions thoroughly – it is very easy for the 'speeches' to be regurgitations straight from the textbook, which exhibit no apparent understanding or which are strings of platitudes or prejudices lacking any sort of reasoning.

We feel that the primary aims with any group at a pre-examination level, should be to awaken interest and to make them aware that Economics is concerned with the real world. The emphasis then, in any work done by the class, should be on finding out for themselves. At this stage the approach need not be dominated by the examination to the same extent that it must be in the examination year. It is not necessary that the end result of the study of every topic on the syllabus be a piece of written work in essay form. Many textbooks offer a selection of exercises which are suitable for work in class or may be used as homework.

Homework and projects

We feel the matter of homework to be important. Where schools insist on homework being given on a particular night in a particular subject, there is a real danger that homework can become something which is tacked on to the lesson and regarded as an imposition by the teacher and class alike. If you try to rationalise your views on homework it may help you to integrate homework into your teaching pattern. You may see it as an opportunity to see how a child works independently, outside the classroom situation. If this is your intention, then try to check up, possibly on parents' nights, how and where the homework is done, as it is easy to be misled as to the extent of the originality or the effort in any piece of work. You may see homework as simply an extension of subject time, giving your class time to do work for which insufficient classtime is available, in which case the homework you set will be no different from any work you may give to be done in class. You may see homework as an opportunity for children to consult other books or other sources of information such as parents, newspapers, radio or television. If you favour this view there is room for the project method which, although it may become time consuming or result in much effort by the teacher and little by the class if it is not carefully planned, does provide opportunities to get individuals involved in finding things out for themselves and, particularly at this 'beginner' stage, it has much to recommend it.

For instance, you might use the project approach to the topic of retailing. Get the class to draw a plan of the local shopping centre. List what shops they find there. Divide the shops between big stores and little stores, multiple shops and single branch shops. You can extend the topic beyond shops. Ask them to plot where the 'big three' banks are situated. Ask them to mark the post office, the police station and other public buildings. You could give a prize for the best town plan. Perhaps you might obtain a large-scale wall plan drawn in colour; talk about it and invite the class to suggest why the banks so often occupy the four corners of the busiest crossroads, how small grocers manage to survive in competition with large cut-price supermarkets, why two T.V. dealers may operate in adjoining shops. This sort of work can be a starting point for many topics in Economics. It is of course important to remember all the time that it is only a starting point and much teaching remains to be done. Something less ambitious would involve asking the class to collect advertisements from the papers, noting slogans on posters or on buses or remembering the jingles and patter on T.V. Discuss these points, ask why firms are willing to spend so much money on advertising. This is one starting point for a treatment of the concepts of supply and demand, consumers' behaviour and the role of the entrepreneur.

Aims in the first-year course

There is a danger that in your efforts to interest the class and give them their heads, the first-year Economics course may become too discursive. The first year is the time to instil good habits. The pupil must be taught to observe and read what happens and then to be able to describe economic behaviour and institutions accurately and clearly.

This is also the time to begin teaching numeracy as well as literacy

31

in Economics. At more advanced levels of the subject, a current complaint is that students are inadequately prepared to deal with a mathematical approach to Economics. At this early stage you have a chance to get your pupils used to the idea that many economic concepts are measurable and that scientific methods can be used. For instance, when you are dealing with taxation, make sure that they really understand what is meant by a progressive tax. They tend to say, rightly, that a man pays more tax as he earns more and forget that it is the rate at which he pays which rises. Get them to find out actual rates of income tax and allowances and to work out examples of tax paid under varying personal circumstances.

Try a little elementary statistics. Show your pupils how to read a table of figures and explain the principles on which it is constructed. Get them to collect examples of graphs and to construct graphs themselves. Point out examples of misleading graphs. Above all, show them how misleading averages can be and say how statisticians are always concerned to give an indication of the accuracy of any figure they produce. A study of the stock market provides a splendid opportunity for using techniques of teaching about stocks and shares with which the class is probably familiar from its Mathematics lessons. It may be possible here to collaborate with the Mathematics department and for you, or your class, to produce examples which can be used whenever the topic is first introduced in the Mathematics syllabus.

There is such a wide range of possible school situations in which Economics may be first introduced to the timetable, that we could not discuss them all in detail. There is a further complication which arises from the nature of the subject of Economics. It is a 'circular' subject, in the sense that, although all the parts of a course are inter-related, there is no obvious starting point and no obligatory order of dealing with topics. We feel, however, that it may be helpful to offer two different teaching syllabuses, to indicate the kind of approaches that have been found successful in the classroom.

Syllabus A. The Economics of everyday life
(A five-term C.S.E. syllabus for fourth and fifth years.)

1. *The T.V. commercial.* Contrasts between goods frequently advertised and those never advertised. Some ideas about competition, about capital and consumer goods, and about the economics of advertising. Forms of nonprice competition.

2. *The advertiser*. Branded products. Resale price maintenance and its control by the state. The advertiser of branded products as a monopolist. Some ideas about the nature of demand, elasticity of demand, and shifts in demand.

Project: a survey of T.V. advertising over a given period.

3. *The consumer*. The effect on the consumer and on demand in general of a successful advertising campaign. The possibility of expenditure on other goods being reduced (or increased, if in joint demand), or of successful advertising acting as an incentive to earn more.

4. *The shopkeeper and the consumer*. A survey of distribution channels. Retailing, wholesaling, mail order and hire purchase. Other forms of credit trading. Supermarkets and small shops; some ideas about economies of scale.

Project: a survey of local shops, noting forms of ownership and commodities sold.

5. *The chain of production and distribution*. How efforts to meet increased demand for one commodity will affect the supply of others; how workers in many different sectors of the economy – in transport, manufacturing industry, in agriculture and mining – may be affected.

6. *Local industry and commerce*. A survey of firms in the school's neighbourhood, and of economic activity in general. A comparison, if possible, with some other well-known area, e.g. a popular holiday resort. Trade directories and the classified telephone directories. The classification of firms according to size, numbers employed, volume of turnover, or type of ownership.

Project: a survey of local job opportunities for school leavers.

7. *Starting in business*. The one-man firm; the problems involved in starting a business. Fixed and working capital and trade credit. The growth of firms through the reinvestment of profits. Some elementary ideas about book-keeping: profit and loss accounts, balance sheets, etc. Identification of the various costs of production, and their division into fixed and variable.

8. *The size and efficiency of firms*. The present trend toward bigger firms. Mergers and take-over bids. The idea of rationalisation – the work of the Industrial Reorganisation Corporation. The attitude of the state – the Monopolies Commission. Are big firms always efficient firms? Are the benefits arising from larger units of production always passed on to the consumer? Nationalised industries and public enterprise.

9. *The Location of firms*. Factors influencing the location of local industries. A survey of the principal industrial areas in the U.K., and the location of some major industries. The development areas and the 'grey' areas and the efforts made by the Board of Trade to influence the location of industry.

Project: special studies of local industries; origins, sources of raw materials, markets, etc.

10. *The young worker*. A. *Finding a job;* the Youth Employment Officer and the Employment Exchange. Apprenticeship schemes and methods of training. The Industrial Training Act. Wages – time and piecework rates, bonuses and incentive schemes. Fringe benefits and luncheon vouchers. The wage packet, P.A.Y.E., National Insurance Contributions, and 'take home pay'.

B. *Protection of the worker by the state;* the Truck Act, the Catering Wages Act, Wages Councils and minimum wage regulations, the Factory and Shops Acts and the work of the Factory Inspectorate.

C. *The organisation of work* within a factory: chargehands, overseers and foremen; management. Types of workers' organisations – the trade union movement and the Trades Union Congress. Wage negotiations, joint consultation, arbitration and conciliation in industrial disputes. The work of a union branch secretary and district organiser.

33

11. *Spending and saving.* A. *Spending* – a recapitulation of some points already covered in sections 1–4. The 'teen-age market' – its importance today compared with the 1930s. Settling transactions; methods of transmitting money over distances. Postal and money orders; the cheque system; the G.P.O.'s Giro and the banks' credit transfer.

B. *Saving.* The merits of different methods of saving compared. The institutions involved: the savings and commercial banks, building societies and insurance companies, etc. A discussion of the services these provide for the consumer (see articles in *Money Which?*).

Projects: a history of money; the changeover to decimal coinage; investing a pools' win.

12. *Taxation.* Another reference to P.A.Y.E. and income tax. Other forms of taxation. An examination of the motorcyclist as a taxpayer. The Budget; reasons for the imposition of taxes; an outline of Government expenditure particularly as it affects the young wage-earner. The public services; rates and local authorities.

13. *Prosperity and the future.* How can we enjoy rising standards of living? How average standards of living are determined by the size of the population and of the national income. An approach to the concept of national income – its distribution as between different factors of production and between different income groups, before and after tax.

A. *The importance of the size and efficiency of the working population.* Factors affecting its size. Ratios of working to total population. The efficient deployment of the working population; the mobility of labour.

B. *The importance of overseas trade* in maintaining employment and adding to the national income. International competitiveness. Our dependence on imported goods. Principal types of exports and the leading export industries. The Government's concern with overseas trade. The balance of trade and the balance of payments.

C. *The importance of maintaining full employment.* A comparison of the 1920s and 30s with the 1950s and 60s. Ways in which the state may help to maintain a high level of employment.

D. *The importance of keeping prices stable.* The dangers and disadvantages of inflation. 'Real' and money wages and the cost of living. Government action – the credit squeeze, 'stop-go'.

E. *The necessity for economic growth,* if the standards of living are to be maintained or increased. The work of the Department of Economic Affairs and of the National Economic Development Council. The difficulties of reconciling these different objectives. The economic problem – that of scarcity and choice.

Syllabus B. The Economics content of a course for 'O' level Economic and Public Affairs

(This is a two-year course, beginning in the fourth year. The subject matter is covered twice.)

1. *Work.* Why men work – division of labour – determination of wages – supply and demand for labour – trade unions – employers' federations – who works (population).

2. *How people spend money.* Consumers' behaviour – supply and demand analysis, price theory – standard of living – cost of living. National income (simple idea of flow) – retail trade.

3. *How industry is organised.* The employer's side – business units – large scale and small scale – location of industry – nationalisation – mergers – changing patterns – role of the entrepreneur.

4. *Money.* Functions – types – history – banking system – insurance – Stock Exchange.

5. *International trade* (sometimes omitted in the fourth year). Advantages and disadvantages – organisation – visible and invisible trade – currency and exchange – devaluation.

6. *The Government and the Economy.* Taxation – grants and subsidies – Government revenue and expenditure – the Budget – other financial controls – other Government controls and influence – prices and incomes policy – monopolies.

These two syllabuses highlight one special problem of approach: whether to spread the course out over two years as in the first case, or to go 'twice round the track', as in the second case. Teachers will have to decide on their own approach; both methods have been proved to work.

As a final comment on the teaching of Economics to beginners, we would like to offer a few examples of how some topics have actually been taught by some of the present authors.

In general we find it desirable to relate things to the pupil's own experience, whilst seeking all the time to widen this experience. Rather than going straight to industry for examples, try to find out what knowledge of industry individuals within the class may have. You will usually find a wide variety of parents' occupations, and occasionally boys are very knowledgeable about these occupations. You could well begin by drawing on their home and school life for examples.

On the basic problem of choice, for instance, ask the class if there are any things they want very much and cannot have. Ask them if their parents have explained why they cannot have these things. Let them make lists of so far unattainable pleasures, like going off on a winter sports holiday at Christmas or a sea voyage in the spring. Get them to look further behind the answer, 'We can't afford it'.

When dealing with the wide topic of labour and wages, you might begin by asking the class to list as many jobs as possible – try to get them to group the jobs by qualifications and earnings. Use the personal approach, 'What job do you want when you leave school?' and determine what influences these choices. Move on to look at how wages are determined. Get them to try their hands at job evaluation and say how they would pay different jobs. It is an easy step from here to the influence of trade unions and their history and structure, or to government intervention in the economy.

35

When you come to money, make things as simple as you can. Ask them to make out a shopping list and insist that they find out the current prices. Give them the prices they would have had to pay 20 years ago and 40 years ago. Collect documents, either genuine or facsimile, such as cheques, postal orders, bills of exchange and treasury bills; make up the documents yourself if you cannot obtain them easily. You can explain why the gold standard would be more efficient than a goat standard. In dealing with banking, you have to explain the difference between the moral advice to young people to live within their means and not get into debt and the situation of the businessman who must borrow if he is to buy new machinery or re-paint his shop. You have to teach that the main purpose of a bank is to lend to its customers at a lucrative rate of interest. It is essential to avoid discussing this sort of thing in a dry-as-dust objective fashion which will bore the class – try making a story out of it. Describe the bank manager's office, the sort of securities which the apprehensive customer will offer and so on. This may be an opportunity to try role-playing with different members of the class taking the parts of the manager and the customer. It is also a good topic to illustrate with a film, since many young people have never actually been inside a bank and the whole business is something of a mystery to them.

B. ECONOMICS IN THE FIFTH FORM

Work with the fifth year will vary according to the organisation of the school. You may continue to work with the same G.C.E. or C.S.E. class that you taught in the fourth year or you may find yourself taking over a class from someone else. Your objectives, methods and scheme of work will have to be modified accordingly, and will always have to be considered in relation to the ability range of those you teach. What follows is written on the assumption that your class has already tackled some Economics in its fourth year, and that it is preparing for some form of examination at the end of the fifth year.

Some teachers find this a difficult assignment because they are forced to consider examination requirements and are, at the same time, dealing with boys and girls at an awkward stage in their development. They have often lost much of their pre-adolescent enthusiasm for school, and have not yet come to terms with themselves as they will in the sixth form or as young adults. Sometimes they work less well than they did in the fourth form but the demands of the approaching examination may well act as a spur to additional effort. Once again you will need to think carefully about your scheme of work, your specific aims and the methods by which your aims are to be achieved.

Your class is no longer new to the subject. They will have acquired some factual knowledge and elementary theory in the fourth year. They will have begun to take notes, to write short answers calling for clear and accurate descriptions – for example, of ordinary and preference shares, and of debentures – or explanations of the different meanings of the word 'dividend' when used on the balance sheets of joint stock companies and cooperative societies. You hope that by this time they have begun to take an interest in newspapers and in T.V. news and discussion programmes. In short, you are continuing to build on foundations which were laid the previous year.

What are your objectives?

At this stage it is easy to be overawed by the approaching G.C.E. examination, or even by the trial examinations which may be held early in the spring term. Teaching is a far-ranging activity, and the worth of a teacher cannot be judged by his 'success' or 'failure' in a small part of his work. Of course, we assume that you want your boys and girls to be successful at 'O' level, but we do not believe this should be your sole or even your primary objective. Your concern is with education. In Economics, you are teaching boys and girls about the world outside which they will soon enter: you are helping them to understand something of the economic system and to widen their outlook and understanding. At the same time, you are trying to teach them to think logically and systematically about quite commonplace phenomena.

You ask them about a firm's profits, and what the size of these profits depend on. You call for a definition of profits, and they realise that since profits represent the difference between total costs and total revenue, they may increase even when total costs are rising – or may decrease when total revenue is increasing. You ask them about the profit on a single article, and you help them to distinguish between total profit and average profit, and to work out the relationship of average profit to total profit. 'If a firm is making a profit of £100 a week, and it doubles its output, will it make a profit of £200?' This is a simple question, quite intelligible to the non-economist, yet impossible to answer unless the nature of profits is understood and their dependence on price, cost, and output.

Again, in discussing firms, the problem of classifying them will arise. Soon it becomes clear that they can be arranged according to the type of product: engineering firms, textile firms, plastics firms and so on. The class may suggest arranging them according to type of ownership: if an attempt is made to arrange them by order of 'size', your class will soon find that the term is imprecise. Is size measured by floor area, by turnover, or by numbers employed? You may point out that another standard of comparison is the capital employed. In this type of discussion you are encouraging your class to think more deeply and more precisely about commonplace topics. So much of the subject matter of Economics is already familiar to the boy or girl and does not have to be 'learned' and it is this which distinguishes Economics from some other school subjects. The very familiarity of the subject matter emphasises the need for a much more rigorous approach to it than to other subjects. Huxley's remark about science being organised common sense might be adapted by all Economics teachers: much elementary Economics is organised, systematised general knowledge.

Your objectives are to impart some factual information, to train your pupils to approach what they know already, and what they learn, in a systematic and logical fashion, whilst continuing to help them to express themselves clearly both orally and in writing.

The content of the course

At this stage you should consider the syllabus of your G.C.E. board and the type of questions which it sets. Past question papers are often a more satisfactory guide to the level of factual knowledge which examiners expect and to the emphasis which they place on different aspects of Economics, than is the syllabus itself. Some topics are included in syllabuses and seem to be regularly ignored when questions are set. Conversely questions are often set apparently without reference to the syllabus. We do not suggest that you build your course on an analysis of the most frequently recurring questions;

we merely point out that in a two-year course you will be able to deal with a limited number of topics, and these at an elementary level. If you are concerned with education as opposed to instruction, with training in logical thinking and analysis, then the actual content of your course is not of paramount importance; how you teach, rather than what you teach, is the major issue. Let the content of your course be influenced, but not determined, by the demands of the examiners; the requirements of the various boards differ, and this implies differences of emphasis in your treatment of certain topics.

We have concentrated, in this section, on the problem of preparing for G.C.E. examinations. You may be working for C.S.E.; much of what has been written will still hold good if your pupils are being examined under Modes A and B. If you have chosen to examine under Mode C (S), then you will be able to relate the content of the course much more closely to the interests and experience of your class. The organisation, structure and problems of local industries may well assume a greater importance and a more central position in your course. Your treatment of such topics as overseas trade and public finance may be more selective, concentrating on those aspects which most closely concern your class. There is a useful note on C.S.E. Economics by F. Davies in *Teaching Economics*, published by the Economics Association and a more detailed study is being prepared for the Association by T. K. Robinson on Economics courses for the less academic pupil.

Syllabuses and schemes of work

The syllabuses of G.C.E. boards tend to follow a conventional pattern, often beginning with problems of scarcity and choice and ending with public finance and international trade. In drawing up your scheme of work, don't follow the subject matter of the syllabus or the order in which topics are dealt with in the syllabus too closely. Suggestions for a two-year course have been made in the preceding chapter: there are other examples of pupil-centred schemes in *Teaching Economics*, in the section contributed by Powicke. In the fifth year, you may wish to return to topics which you dealt with in the previous year – the 'twice round the track' treatment – as well as to deal with fresh material.

A class will normally appreciate a logical and connected approach.

It is as well to prepare your scheme of work well in advance, perhaps dividing the school year into six half terms, and making a rough division of the subject matter accordingly, making some allowance for examination time and for revision. It is a common fault to attempt to cover too much ground. It is better that your class should learn and understand a limited amount than that the syllabus should be covered yet not understood. Be flexible in your approach: be ready to modify the content or timing of your course if the class finds a particular topic more difficult – or for that matter, more interesting – than usual.

Fifth year teaching methods

In this fifth year you will probably find it useful to go over basic ideas a second time and make sure the class have not only learnt definitions but, more important, understood them and can express them in their own words. Tackle again the concepts which they found difficult the previous year. If, for example, you are dealing with the Stock Exchange again, you will give more time to analysing its functions and less to description. By all means let the class have in their minds the picture of the broker in his bowler hat, the garb of respectability, as they may need an image at this point, but do impress upon them that in the end the great virtue of the Stock Exchange is that it is a free market in existing securities which it thereby endows with liquidity. As a result the capital market is able to attract the savings of the public with new issues and so provide industry with new capital.

Your class may already have begun to collect press cuttings. Now is the time to encourage a more selective approach to these cuttings; to be more critical and systematic in their attitude. They will have begun to take notes: encourage them to cultivate the art of note-taking and to avoid the lengthy précis they often make. You may find it necessary to dictate a short note from time to time – say, the distinction between the balance of payments and the balance of trade, or the definition of bank rate.

At this stage they will rely a good deal on their textbook. Encourage them to bring some of the information in it up to date; government policy towards the location of industry or towards the growth of monopolies may have altered since it was published. Individual fifth formers can often make intelligent use of the Department of Economic Affairs broadsheets and progress reports; if it seems probable that they will continue to study Economics in the sixth form, you might encourage them to buy such paperbacks as Donaldson's *Guide to the British Economy* (Penguin) and Williams' *Economics of Everyday Life* (Penguin) and suggest sections of other books which they might read. Some firms issue brochures, and if you hand out to each boy and girl copies of the study booklets (published by the Bank Education Service and issued free to schools) on, for example, the clearing house, or the National Coal Board's booklet *Coal in Britain Today* – again, free on request – you are supplementing the textbook, encouraging wider reading, and possibly introducing the idea of books as personal possessions. It may be possible for you to build up a classroom bookshelf, and this could include such 'fringe' reading as Quiggin, *The Story of Money* (Methuen Outlines), Ferris *The City* (Penguin) and vol. vii of the Oxford Junior Encyclopaedia, *Industry and Trade*.

Treat television as an ally rather than as an enemy. Its potentialities as a medium of education have yet to be realised. Men or women who play an important part in economic affairs, the Chancellor of the Exchequer, many leading industrialists and trade union secretaries, the chairmen of nationalised industries and the general secretary of the T.U.C., are often featured on news and discussion programmes, and the fifth form boy or girl may well be able to recognise many of them. Press photographs may be used for a class quiz. This is something new – the 'Chancellor of the Exchequer' is ceasing to be an abstract concept to millions of boys and girls of school age, but the man they saw on the news the previous day, leaving Downing Street for the House, and explaining his Budget later in the evening. This development presents teachers with an advantage which they have not possessed in the past, and one which merits serious consideration.

Try to make the work as varied as possible. You might use a lesson occasionally for a discussion or debate; or give the class duplicated extracts from newspaper articles and give them twenty short questions on each – borrow the technique of the English 'comprehension' lesson and adapt it to your purpose. Reports on Stock Exchange proceedings, on the money market, extracts from the chairman's annual report at company meetings, or from politician's speeches, can all be used in this way. Duplicate a couple of pages of notes for them occasionally, to be fastened into their notebooks. This shows them how notes should be made; it allows them to give their whole attention to what you are talking about in class, and makes oral questioning during a lesson much easier.

In the fifth year the ability to produce a written answer to a question will be increasing; introduce your class to the half-hour essay question gradually. Discuss these essay questions thoroughly in class to begin with; make sure everyone understands the question and knows what is expected of him or her. Most of the actual writing will be done as homework, but if you can arrange it, let them practise writing in lesson time within a strict time limit. This is not training solely in examination technique: an ability to write against the clock is something worthwhile in itself which you can help to foster. At the present time all 'O' level examinations still require essay-type answers; the essay is essentially a literary form, accepted over the years as the orthodox means of expression of literary or historical ideas and opinions; it is assumed, possibly without much reason, that a knowledge and understanding of Economics is best tested in this way too. It is strange that we should claim that Economics is a social science, yet have done little to make use of the techniques used by the teachers of the physical sciences to test knowledge and understanding.

If you are dealing with stocks and shares, or yields and dividends, for example, set some simple numerical questions calling for a manipulation of figures and a use of simple formulae.

What is the yield on a £1 ordinary share if the market price is £1·25 and the dividend 10%?

If a banker observes a cash ratio of 8% and his till money and balance at the Bank of England together amount to £150 millions, how big will his liabilities be?

Questions of this type preclude the copying out of definitions or paraphrases of sections of the textbook, and are often effective in revealing misunderstandings and misconceptions.

When you return the written work to the class explain how you mark and why Black has done well and White not so well: make sure Gray knows where he was irrelevant and that Brown understands that his afterthought earned him another three or four marks. Boys and girls like these post-mortems and they begin to realise their homework has not been invented to keep them indoors at night but is a worthwhile activity in itself. Teachers are often thorough and conscientious in preparing lessons and marking homework, yet curiously thoughtless about the homework itself. When you set homework, do consider its content and purpose. Routine copying up of notes, or paraphrasing sections of textbook, will soon kill interest in the subject. Try to set a task which is interesting in itself, and which makes some intellectual demands on the boy or girl. Do not make it too hard or too long: if the work is interesting, more time will be spent on it anyway. Simple reading assignments tend to be done badly because at this stage the average fifth former will not have learnt to think carefully about what he is reading. It is better to duplicate a list of questions, each to be answered by a sentence, based on a page or two of the textbook; this will involve you in more preparation, but it is more effective.

Try to visualise the home circumstances of those you teach, and don't assume they are all adequately housed and have access to encyclopaedias and reference books. Many of them will be snatching a corner of the kitchen table while the rest of the family eat or talk against a background of Radio 2.

4

THE SIXTH FORM

A. ADVANCED LEVEL ECONOMICS

It is assumed that the group in the lower sixth has taken 'O' level in several subjects with varying degrees of success. Increasingly the Economics sixth is attracting students with a broad range of ability and widely differing ambitions. Such a group may well include potential honours graduates in Economics, others hoping to pursue professional studies after a sixth form course (perhaps realising that they may be exempt from certain professional examinations with an 'A' level pass in Economics), while the remainder may include those hoping to secure additional 'O' level passes. Some students in the group will have taken 'O' level in Economics, others will not. The most workable solution may well prove to be to assume that no one has studied the subject and to start from fundamentals.

The syllabus

We now turn to a more general consideration of the 'A' level course. You, the teachers, are faced with a dilemma because you have two years in which to cover the ground. Are you going to cover the syllabus slowly over the two years or are you going to cover the work in a shorter period, say three or four terms and then revise for the remaining time? On these approaches, opinions differ; and there is no weight of evidence or particularly powerful argument which suggests that one method is better than another. It is a matter of choice whether you spend five terms of the 'A' level course teaching fully each topic as you come to it, leaving one term for revision at the end of the course; or four terms detailed study and two terms revising the main topics; or the 'twice round the clock' method, with a first year outline course and a second year examining the subject in greater depth. The organisation of the second year course is complicated by having to 'bring the pupils to the boil' at the right times. In addition to the 'A' level examination proper many schools have trial G.C.E. examinations in the spring term, and some schools enter pupils for the pre-'A' level 'Oxbridge' entrance examinations in the autumn term. Time must be set aside for revision in class and allowance must be made on your teaching schedule if your school permits pupils to go home to prepare for examinations or gives them extra private time in the library.

Whatever the arrangements are, you will require a school syllabus to suit your own needs. This should be a comprehensive scheme of work providing a complete unified course in which subjects are introduced in a logical sequence. It may correspond in outline to the syllabus provided by the examining board but will be in much more detail; additional topics may be included and your sequence for dealing with the topics may be different from that of the board. It is helpful if each student has a copy of the school syllabus: this serves as a guide to where he is going in the next two years and in the later stages of the course it serves as a reminder of where he has been.

The traditional approach to teaching 'A' level Economics is to begin with micro-economics and end with macro-economics. Many teachers adopt this approach simply because it is traditional and because most textbooks follow this order. It is perhaps worthwhile to examine the advantages and disadvantages of reversing the order.

Macro-economics has the attraction of being relevant. Many pupils who choose to take Economics do so because their interest has been aroused by the emphasis on economic affairs which the mass media present. They would like to know more about the balance of payments problem, or about the significance of the un-employment level, or about the incomes policy. It can be disconcerting to spend a couple of terms as an 'A' level Economics student and still be no more informed on these matters than before starting the course. If teachers of Economics are asked to provide short courses for General Studies pupils in the sixth form, the topics already mentioned are likely to figure prominently.

The difficulty in beginning an 'A' level Economics course in this way is that the teacher expects a deeper understanding from his 'A' level pupils than he does from his General Studies pupils. In dealing with 'A' level candidates, the teacher will probably feel it is necessary to put in lengthy asides about consumers' behaviour or the theory of the firm, which may make the approach very diffuse.

45

This problem of 'macro versus micro' approach, is in essence the difference between two contrasting views in Educational Psychology. On the one hand there is the 'gestalt' approach of presenting a wide picture and allowing pupils to pick out interrelated patterns for themselves, which corresponds roughly to the 'macro first' approach. On the other hand is the atomised approach, where the parts of the picture are presented to the pupil systematically and built up into the whole, which corresponds roughly to the 'micro first' approach.

As always, of course, a compromise is possible. One which many teachers use is to begin teaching a micro framework but to follow up economic events as they are happening and use them as an introduction to macro-economics, which is then developed systematically at a later stage in the course. Another possibility is to begin an 'A' level course by giving the class the kind of brief outline macro course which a General Studies class would receive, with no asides or extensions, and then revert to the traditional 'micro first' approach.

In drawing up the course for the year it is doubtful if there is but one ideal order of topics. Economics is a 'circular' subject, and so there are several suitable starting points. Some teachers begin with the economic problems, others with money and banking, and others with macro-economics. The teacher may have decided to follow the order in the textbook the class is using when organising the course. It is as well to adopt a logical sequence so that each new topic builds on the framework of fundamental concepts established in teaching the previous topic. Some teachers have found the following a helpful sequence:

The economic problem→the factors of production→specialisation→large-scale production→the equilibrium of the firm→monopoly→consumer behaviour→demand and supply→the theory of distribution→inflation→value of money→money and banking→international trade→government policy→macro-economics →regional development

Wherever you start it is important that during the formative period the basic concepts are taught thoroughly. Make sure that your class understands such concepts as the theory of comparative costs, and opportunity cost, and the significance of the assumption of 'other things being equal'. Unless the pupil comes from a poor home he will not yet have the experience of life that brings home to him the existence of relative scarcity; it is worth spending a few days illustrating how our everyday lives are dominated by scarcity. Use examples from the school situation: the alternative uses to which the ground on which the school stands could have been put, balanced against the social value of the school; the limitations on the number of combinations of subjects which may be taken in the sixth form; the reasons for the lack of equipment such as a television set or a computer which would be useful teaching aids; the shortage of expensive books in the form library. Once you have made the point, go further from home and compare the peasant in an Indian village with the average citizen of the United States. You could contrast the obvious affluence of Britain, judging by the shops and lights and cars, with the fact that we had to devalue the pound in 1967 and had to be austere in our spending.

The next two years are going to be spent looking at problems with the background of scarcity, so it is time well employed if this background is never forgotten. Try to think of unusual examples of opportunity costs. We can go to watch Tottenham Hotspur play Manchester United or Chelsea play Liverpool, we can't do both, which is it to be? We can watch 'Dixon of Dock Green' or 'Match of the Day', but not both. These are dilemmas which they can appreciate and they bring home the real significance of these otherwise academic concepts.

Reading

The sixth former must be taught to read a book quickly. This is an art and the young student needs guidance. He tends to read too slowly because he tries to learn things by heart; he must be persuaded not to do this, but to bookmark any passage he thinks important. He can come back to it, read it again, perhaps make a note about it, and ask you to explain it to him. He must not 'dog-ear' a page, as this is almost sacrilege; books deserve greater respect. He must read widely and above all know his basic textbooks from cover to cover. From the beginning of the lower sixth the students should be encouraged to build up a library of their own. By buying paperbacks like Donaldson's *Guide to the British Economy*, Jan Pen's *Modern Economics* and Stewart's *Keynes and After*, they will soon have a small but effective group of supplementaries. In their choice of such books they will need considerable help and advice.

Textbooks

The problem of textbooks arises from the outset. This is a matter for personal judgment: all we would say is that whereas some teachers prefer to issue only one Economics textbook to the first-year sixth there are those who would rather the students used two or three covering much the same ground. It is helpful to have several sets of useful textbooks and books on specialist topics readily available in the Economics room, and to persuade the class to build up their own library of paperbacks. In addition the department should have a supply of relatively expensive books like Lipsey's *Positive Economics* or Samuelson's *Economics* which small groups should share. Finance sets a limit on both these ideas. Pupils should be reminded that the statistics in textbooks are usually out of date and it is necessary to extract current figures from Government publications, bank reviews, and newspapers. (A list of these is given elsewhere.) These figures are not for learning by heart, but for the quantitative ideas they suggest, and the economic perspective they create.

Notes

There are few things we can do for our pupils that will be of greater practical use to them than to teach them how to take notes. Apart from the work they will do for us, most of them will be going on either to formal further education or to studying for occupational or professional examinations. They will need to take notes both from the books they read and the lessons or lectures they listen to. Yet how many students in their first year at university have a satisfactory technique of note-taking?

The first essential is to decide what purpose we want notes to serve. We would suggest the following three functions:

(1) to provide a permanent record,

(2) to be as short yet as comprehensive a record as possible,

(3) to afford easy reference.

If the notes are to be permanent, they should always be well written and well set out. In the case of lecture or class notes, it may take nearly as long to rewrite and reshape the notes as the original lesson or lecture took but the time is well spent. Not only is a well-organised and easy-to-read set of notes obtained, but during the rewriting which should also be a rethinking, a revision takes place at the time when most forgetting occurs – within the first twenty-four hours.

It is important to establish at the start the difference between essay English and notes. To begin with, most of our pupils will write too many words. They will write 'It is important to remember the Limited Liability Act of 1855 . . . " In note form, 'nb Ltd. Liability 1855' is enough. Not only do unnecessary words take time to write, but they rob the notes of their impact and ease of quick reference.

If notes are to serve the purpose of affording quick reference, they need to be well set out under headings and sub-headings, and often sub-sub-headings. The advertising layout experts have a lot to teach us. They do not mind leaving spaces blank if it adds to the impact of what they have to say. A heading should always stand nearer to the left-hand margin than any of the writing under that heading. In this way the heading is made to stand out boldly. Underlining can help and so can the use of colours.

Should notes be dictated? We believe they should not, with the exception of quotations and some of the important definitions during the early stages. Notes should, in fact, be the unique joint product of the mind of the teacher (or writer) and the mind of the taught. Thus, no two sets of notes should be identical.

However, if we are to teach them the art of note-taking they must have guidance. This can be given by writing on the blackboard the numbered, or lettered, headings and sub-headings of what we intend to talk about during the lesson. This will lay down guidelines and they can develop their own notes under the headings. Again, we do not want essay writing under the headings but rather we want them to analyse what is said into separate numbered, or lettered, points.

The following headings will serve as an example. They cover ground that might occupy several periods according to the time at our disposal and how deeply we want to go into the subject. We might decide to give a whole period to, say heading (4) (b) (i), with examples from the High Street, discussion of tied public houses, petrol station franchise, and so on. Even if we do take a subject in some detail, they will not lose sight of the wood for the trees so long as the argument is kept under the main headings.

(Example)
THE SIZE OF FIRMS
I. *Large firms*
  (1) *Large firms in British industry*
  (2) *Internal and external economies*
  (3) *The advantages of scale*
    (a) Technical
    (b) Managerial
    (c) Buying and selling
    (d) Financial
    (e) Risk bearing
  (4) *How firms grow larger*
    (a) Horizontal integration
    (b) Vertical integration
      (i) Forward toward the consumer
      (ii) Backward toward the raw materials
    (c) Diversification
    (and so on . . .)

Essays

You will find, unless you are exceptionally lucky, that many of your pupils need to be taught the use of English and the technique of essay writing. When setting an essay it is wise to make a few suggestions as to how it should be approached, along with a good reading list, and adequate class notes. Why should you allow the pupil to waste his time and yours by writing a lot of irrelevant material? Don't allow them to copy sections out of books or simply repeat without thought, their own class notes. Insist that they write out the full question at the head of the essay. This will help to concentrate the question in their minds and reduce irrelevance. Even the obvious point that there must be a beginning, a middle and an end, should be stressed. It is often forgotten that the assumptions on which the essay is based must be made clear at the start. In the opening paragraph should occur the essential definitions required in the answer such as 'The multiplier measures the effect of an injection of expenditure on the equilibrium level of national income. This expenditure becomes additional income to the various factors of production and the size of the multiplier depends on the relative proportions of this additional income which are saved and consumed, i.e. the marginal propensities to save and to consume.'

You can usefully spend a period handing back essays, going over in detail the faults which have appeared and working out, in discussion with the class, the main points which were needed. You will probably find that time is too short to do this with every essay, but much can be done to improve the standard of essay writing by making useful comments in the margin, and in your conclusion. This will involve you in a lot of hard work, but your industry will be repaid. You should take trouble to produce consistent standards and a meaningful marking system, which will give the pupil a realistic idea of his progress towards 'A' level.

Model answers

When you have been through a topic with the class it pays to do some relevant exercises on the blackboard or overhead projector, going through some examination questions and building up model answers. These models are merely guides and not to be learnt by heart as 'cribs'. You must emphasise that this is not the aim of the model at all. What you are trying to do is to show the class how a question might be answered so that they themselves have a method, an apparatus of thinking to apply to their problems. They must think about those problems and write their solutions to them in their own words.

Methods and objectives

Your pupils may well have difficulty in understanding ideas which are outside their experience but it is as well to introduce them to difficult concepts while their minds are fresh and impressionable. If you show confidence in them you will be surprised at their response. The transformation in the second-year sixth is often astonishing; your young economists have suddenly started to make sensible value judgments; the mysteries of macro-economics are no longer insoluble.

It is surely as important to stimulate interest in the subject as it is to prepare for examinations. The pupil who continues to take a lively interest in economic affairs after leaving school and the pupil who chooses a career in some related field through his interest in the subject is as much your success as the pupil with a good 'A' level pass. A further object of the course should be to continue a wide education in the subject. The teacher should not be so bound by the 'A' level syllabus that he is unable to pursue an interesting topic beyond these requirements. Current news items often provide an excellent opportunity to educate the class in the wider significance of the subject. A fundamental aim in teaching any subject in the sixth form is to provide an academic discipline. One of the strongest arguments for teaching Economics is the first-rate training it offers in the use of logic, in precise thinking and in the expression of ideas clearly and concisely.

The methods adopted to fulfil these objectives should include a mixture of formal and informal techniques. The greater part of your teaching will probably consist of the formal classroom methods, usually described as 'chalk and talk'. The value of the carefully prepared lesson with the pupils genuinely involved in its development has been demonstrated by centuries of experience. The theoretical side of Economics lends itself well to the Socratic method of building up the lesson on a series of well-chosen questions. In this way the class will come to see the logical sequences which are at the heart of Economic theory. On the descriptive side of the subject the main aim of the teacher is to put across the factual information essential to an understanding of the economic scene. There is a great deal of this work which the pupil can do for himself with some guidance on where to look for the material. It is a problem especially relevant to the Economics teacher that the essential factual material of the subject must continually be revised and brought up to date. The lecture method is probably the easiest way to put across this information, but unsupported by other aids to learning this method has been shown to be very inefficient. It is vital that the pupils learn to take adequate notes during such a lecture, or that you provide them with a duplicated summary of the main points. Even at this stage in their school career it is necessary to test the pupils frequently to assess their assimilation of important facts and concepts. Several of the standard textbooks (e.g. Lipsey, Nevin) have accompanying workbooks which are designed to test and supplement the pupils' understanding of the text. Multiple choice testing will be playing a bigger part in the examining of the subject in the future, and it is a valuable way of testing the pupils' understanding. You can design your own programme-test by duplicating sentences with key words or phrases missing to be completed by the pupil. A detailed treatment of objective testing and the use of workbooks is given in chapter 5.

Other ways of stimulating interest and widening the scope of the subject are discussed at length elsewhere. Visits to the local factories, markets and banks, or if you are near London, to the Stock Exchange the Bank of England and Lloyd's, help you to catch the interest of your class. They also give the pupils the chance to see on the ground what you have been talking about in class and they have been reading about in books. These visits need careful preparation and follow-up. The use of the project system either in conjunction with a visit or to cover a major topic is becoming more widespread. With the help of a detailed bibliography prepared by the teacher the pupil carries out a study in depth of some particular topic and writes it up in say 4,000 words. The pupils could work in pairs, each pair covering a different industry. The projects can be passed around the set and duplicated summaries provided. If there is time a lecture on each of the best project topics can be given by the pupils. In this way a whole range of industries can be covered with great economy of time.

Homework

We are obviously failing as teachers if a great deal of the work on the 'A' level is not done by the pupil himself. Homework must be carefully organised and varied. Note making is an important element and it can take several forms. Rough class notes should be written up but there may not be time for this in the 'A' level year. Class notes should be supplemented with brief notes from or references to textbooks and more detailed work from specialist sources.

Essay questions should be set to be done after the pupils have worked through a reading list. These essays should be either answers of examination length or more exhaustive accounts. Time should be allowed for pupils to work at home on their projects and to keep up diaries and scrapbooks. As a variation on the usual homework you can set simple problems from work books or problems of a mathematical nature or multiple choice questions. Graphical representation of changes in demand and supply conditions, measurement of elasticities, and questions on the equilibrium level of output and price for the firm are a few obvious examples of this type of homework.

Particular problems

Every teacher has his own particular methods of teaching different topics in the Economics course. What works well for one teacher in a given teaching situation may not work for the same teacher in a different situation or for a different teacher in the same situation. Nevertheless we thought it might be helpful to offer some examples of ways in which particular problems might be approached at the sixth-form level.

You can prepare an anatomy of a big firm and put it on the blackboard very effectively. A firm like Unilever or I.C.I. will help you here with wall charts. You can trace the chain of command through the family tree and it becomes apparent, as this chain lengthens and spreads tentacles, that control from the top becomes cumbersome and tedious and that sooner or later the efficiency of management is threatened by size. You should make much of the fact that the entrepreneur capable of, or wishful of, managing a giant firm is rare.

When you come to explain why so many small firms continue to exist in an age of mass production and sophisticated real capital, stress that these firms are dealing with small markets in which personal service counts a lot. In these small markets price is high and demand is inelastic, because the consumer wants something special like a Rolls Royce car or a Savile Row suit or a Paris gown, and is willing to pay for it. The equilibrium size of the firm needs a lot of attention. You must explain that the assumption which the economist makes about the entrepreneur's desire to maximise his profit is a starting point for a theory. Explain perfect competition and imperfect competition; point out in particular that in the former state the factors of production are free to move about in search of greater rewards and that there is only one price so that average revenue, marginal revenue and price are equal; stress the fact that in imperfect competition the firms are unequal in efficiency and so there is a tendency towards oligopoly and then to monopoly. Draw the diagrams on the blackboard that illustrate marginal cost and marginal revenue, average cost and average revenue in both cases. You will find Lipsey particularly useful in doing this (see his *Positive Economics*, second edition). Explain what you mean by competition; the Lawn Tennis Championships at Wimbledon or the Football Association Cup are useful examples because you can show how, in the early stages, the best teams, though they only have eleven players like their opponents, will usually win comfortably. When they meet each other in the later stages they are so evenly matched that the results are very uncertain. The same is true of Wimbledon, the easy victories of seeded players in the early rounds grow into more and more severe 'five set matches' as the quarter-finals draw near and the players are well matched. Big firms in an oligopoly find it pays better to live and let live rather than to indulge in a fierce suicidal struggle. The entrepreneur will, except for the rare Napoleons of industry, prefer to rest on his laurels.

Maximum output for minimum input should be frequently explained. You must get the class to understand that nothing can be produced unless some element of all the factors are employed, the special role of the entrepreneur, the blending of factors in the most productive proportions, the growing use of capital in proportion to labour and land today. Explain the organisation of the firm, the nature of the joint-stock company, the evolution of scientific management at the same time as the individual owner-entrepreneur is disappearing, the cult of efficiency for its own sake. This will provide a good opportunity to discuss again the rate of interest, and marginal efficiency of capital, the practice of large firms of saving part of gross profit, and so on.

The economies and diseconomies of scale are often misunderstood. Explain as clearly as you can that diminishing returns arise from varying proportions in which the factors are employed, whereas diseconomies arise because *all* the factors are not so readily available and are becoming more expensive to employ.

It is inevitable and desirable that you discuss the historical background to economic institutions. By all means encourage your class to read Sir R. Harrod's *A Life of J. M. Keynes* or J. K. Galbraith's *Affluent Society* but also advise them not to waste words in an examination attributing to Keynes or to Marshall something which perhaps they did not say. A paper in Economics is not a paper on the History of Economic Thought. The enthusiastic candidate will find his knowledge of current events runs away with him and instead of confining himself to a discussion of the advantages and disadvantages of devaluation, he will indulge in an irrelevant discussion of whether Mr Wilson or Mr Callaghan were to blame for the United Kingdom's troubles in 1967 or whether they committed some moral crime by going back on promises. The adolescent economist is often an idealist and so he should be. His value judgments are tinged with emotion and coloured with prejudice. Be careful not to disillusion him or to make him think you are a cynic, but try to be as objective as possible yourself and persuade him to do likewise. If he has to tackle a question on whether hospital beds should be paid for according to supply and demand or allocated according to need, he is not expected to answer as an expert who is familiar with all the ins-and-outs of the Ministry of Health's problem, but to bring out the relative scarcity of resources and the significance of opportunity costs. If he uses these concepts and theories with common sense he will write a sound, lucrative answer.

Keep on telling them that it is profitable to understand simple economic analysis and to apply this to a problem as Mr George Schwartz does so delightfully in his weekly article in the *Sunday Times*. For instance the question 'Why does a university professor of Economics earn more than a coal miner whose job is physically hard and dangerous?' does not require the candidate to know what the professor does or what the coalminer does. He needs a little common sense to realise that the supply of professors relative to demand is lower than the supply of coalminers because the special ability of the professor is scarce and educational opportunities are not available to all. You could probably interest them by discussing the economic rent of the Beatles or the scarce talent of a film star like Elizabeth Taylor or a footballer like George Best. You can get them interested in inelasticity of supply if you talk about the black market in tickets for the Cup Final at Wembley or in real costs of production with an unusual question like 'Is there such a thing as a free lunch?' They know that far more people want to watch the Cup Final than there are tickets, that the size of the ground cannot conveniently be increased and that the Football Association is not a profit-making company that is interested in raising prices to the maximum to get the maximum return. You can point out that even if they are taken out to lunch free, even if the host does not have to pay the bill but merely signs it, someone has to pay for it in money terms and a lot of other people have to work in order to provide the materials like meat and vegetables, heat and equipment which were employed. These are the real costs of the meal.

Preparation for 'A' level examinations

At several points in this book we have emphasised that our concern is with education, more especially with the contribution that the teacher of Economics may make to the educational process. Nevertheless, in the sixth form as in the fifth, the Economics teacher is confronted with the problem of external examinations and is subjected to pressures from sixth formers, parents and indeed the school itself to achieve 'good results'.

On the face of things, there appears to be a difference of aims implicit in the use of such contrasted phrases as 'teaching Economics' and 'preparing candidates for the 'A' level examination in Economics', but what is the alternative? Do we ignore external examinations altogether, regarding them as irrelevant, or is there some middle course in which we have to try to balance the demands made by the examiners against our efforts to teach the subject?

Here is a passage from *Education and The Working Class* (Jackson and Marsden, Penguin Books, p. 51). A teacher is talking:

I reckon I can do 'A' level Chem. in four terms. Four terms flat out, mind. We have to go really fast. We have tests twice a week, but we get results. For instance, last year I got an 'open' at Pembroke, Cambridge, and an exhibition at Trinity Hall, Cambridge, and then I got half-a-dozen places. I've got 14 places in the last two years, and then these 'opens'. I do pretty well; my results are all right. The way we teach, we teach for results. I want the passes, the Schools, and all those things. Test all the time, scrub the teaching methods, forget about the educational side. Yes, it is like that; not altogether, of course, but there are two ways, aren't there? There's the one way I teach, and the other way. Well, let me give you an instance: if a boy asks a question it might raise some interesting matters. Now, the other way you'd waste the whole period and follow up those matters and that's all right. But that's not our way. We've got no time for any questions or anything that leads off the syllabus. You've got to go through it. I like teaching our A stream boys, but you should see our C stream! They're shocking, absolutely shocking. I don't like teaching them at all, and I don't know what it can be like in the secondary modern schools . . . Really work these children, tests, tests, tests, and get the results . . . People would know that I could do the job. I might slacken off when I got established – perhaps after ten years or so, I might start looking around and thinking more about the educational side. But you've got to establish yourself first, haven't you? Right.

This to us is deplorable. It is easy to criticise the attitude of the crammer, teaching for results, yet many teachers would feel that it is impracticable to ignore the examinations altogether. While acknowledging the basic aim of developing the sixth former's potentialities and helping him to become a competent economist, they feel that there is also a need for training in 'examination technique' quite unconnected with the subject itself.

The increasing competition for university places and the undue importance which is attached to gaining high grades mean that most

c   57 of us will feel that we should try to make the best of our boys' chances at 'A' level. Is some special preparation for the examination essential? Before answering this question we may pause for a moment and ask what the examiners themselves are trying to do – what their own requirements are: it will then be easier to judge how far these clash with the teacher's aims and to what extent they will force him to modify his aims and methods.

In the first place, examiners will expect some measure of factual knowledge. At 'O' level this will be tested directly, while at 'A' level such knowledge will often be assumed. 'A' level candidates can still expect some questions, or parts of questions, involving descriptive Economics:

Describe the main changes in the size, age – and sex – composition of the population of the U.K. during the past twenty years.

Summarise post-war legislation directed against restrictive practices and monopolies.

Secondly, examiners will try to test knowledge of economic theory and familiarity with certain concepts. Hence a typical question may begin by requiring a definition:

What is understood by the term, 'price elasticity of demand'?
What is economic rent?

or may ask for the statement of some economic principle:

What is meant by 'the law of diminishing returns'?

At 'A' level and beyond examiners will try to assess candidates' ability to apply theory to given situations and their capacity for economic analysis. In seeking to test a candidate's ability to think logically about a problem, the examiners will set such questions as:

What are the likely economic effects of the successful exploitation of North Sea gas?

Is the existence of large numbers of small firms due to the difficulties such firms may have in raising capital?

In so far as the 'A' level examination is a written examination, answering any one of these three types of question will impose a further test on the candidate. This is a test of his ability to read with understanding, to express himself clearly and to communicate with the examiner.

To what extent do you, the teacher, need, to make special preparations to meet the examiners' requirements? You cannot divorce the teaching of Economics from the imparting of factual knowledge and we have given suggestions about the ways in which you can 'put over' factual information to your classes and make the learning process more efficient. You will prepare a scheme of work, give your classes up to date material and test them before moving on to fresh topics.

Similarly with the examiners' demand for some knowledge of economic theory: this will be met by your efforts during the two-year course, however you decide to plan your scheme of work. You will have impressed on your class the importance of learning definitions and of being ready to illustrate a definition with an appropriate example. You may encourage them to practice writing paragraphs on a variety of economic concepts: opportunity cost, diminishing returns, external economics, pure profit and so on. This is not mere cramming for examination purposes. If you are teaching Economics you will want your students to be familiar with economic concepts and to be able to explain them; you will insist on the correct use of such terms as 'cash', and frown on the colloquial use of the word 'money' as a synonym for 'income' or 'profit' in such phrases as 'the speculator makes money by selling shares after they have risen in price'. Frequent testing, both oral and written, is essential: this may be carried out without the setting of formal essays.

It is essential that an 'A' level candidate should be able to apply economic theory to given situations and to think clearly and logically about economic problems. This requirement lies at the heart of much 'A' level work. The writing of essays is the traditional method of both training and testing powers of analysis, but there are other methods, possibly more effective and certainly less time-consuming.

One of these is the setting of questions which involve some manipulation of information, similar in character to a mathematical calculation. To test understanding of the concept of elasticity of demand, as opposed to testing ability to quote a definition, the first step would be to ask:

If the demand for apples is 40 lb at price 5p. and 60 lb at price 4p., will demand be elastic or inelastic?

The object here would be to test understanding of the principle that when total outlay rises after a fall in price, demand is elastic.

59

At a more advanced level the student would use the formula:

$$\text{elasticity of demand} = \frac{\%\ \text{change in quantity}}{\%\ \text{change in price}}$$

to answer such questions as:

What would be the price elasticity of demand for a commodity if a 10% change in price resulted in a 5% fall in the quantity demanded?

If the elasticity of demand for a commodity over a certain price range is 3, what percentage rise in the quantity demanded would follow a 2% fall in price?

The next step would be to test familiarity with, and understanding of the formula:

$$\text{elasticity of demand} = \epsilon = \frac{p.\mathrm{d}q}{q.\mathrm{d}p}$$

and to ask the student to calculate price elasticities of demand over various price ranges on a demand schedule. We have more to say on the techniques of teaching and testing using mathematical concepts in chapter 6, 'Mathematics in Economics'. We think it worthwhile to test the ability to apply a formula in this way as a step beyond the ability to quote a definition. At a later stage refinements can be added so that it is understood that elasticity of demand for a product cannot be seen in isolation but may be affected by changes in taste and fashion, by changes in the prices of other goods and by changes in income.

The great advantage of this type of question is that it is flexible: it is capable of many variations to meet different ranges of ability and experience. It is especially useful in teaching the theory of value, the theory of the firm, the balance of payments and foreign exchange, and macro-economics. The examples above will test more quickly and more accurately an understanding of the concept of elasticity of demand than any formal essay. An important point too in its favour is the speed and ease with which such a question may be marked, and any weakness or lack of understanding exposed. You can make up this type of question yourself, supplementing the many examples in Harvey, or in the workbooks of Nevin, Lipsey and Samuelson. Some examining boards are already including these numerical questions in their papers, but we suggest that this type of question is so useful and effective that you make use of it whether your students are likely to meet it in their 'A' level papers or not.

The traditional essay question tests the ability to think clearly, logically, and precisely. You can achieve the same purpose by the use of 'true or false' problems – ask your sixth formers whether a given statement is true or false, and make them give a short explanation of the reasons for their answer.

If the amount of money in circulation were doubled, the country's wealth would also double.
The optimum firm is that which is maximising its profits.
At the equilibrium level of national income, all resources are fully employed.

Like the numerical questions these 'true or false' questions quickly expose misunderstanding and uncertainties and preclude the copying out of material from textbooks or notes. As with the other types of questions, practice by students may be oral or written and you will find that you can prepare such questions to cover a wide range of topics. Practice in answering this type of question is valuable, irrespective of whether it is likely to be encountered in 'A' or 'S' level examination papers.

Finally, we come to the problem of the candidate's ability to express himself and to communicate by the written word with the examiner. The candidate at advanced level is usually expected to write a series of four or five essay-type answers in a period of from two and a half to three hours. What is frequently called 'coaching for "A" level' is usually the result of the teacher's fears about his candidates' ability to pass this last test: hence the instructions on examination technique that are so often referred to, the attempts to 'spot' questions and the dictating of prepared model answers.

If your teaching (and testing) has been organised around your candidates, rather than directed towards the examination, most of these attempts to beat the examiners will be unnecessary. One or two special requirements of the essay – a literary form of expression, as has been pointed out elsewhere – may be noted, however.

Instil the need to read the question carefully, to analyse it and to answer all of it. Questions are often mis-read or misunderstood through hasty reading and, when there is a main question followed by a supplementary question, the latter is often forgotten. Every chief examiner's report laments the fact that candidates tend to pick on a familiar word or phrase and proceed to say all they know about it with the result that their answers are irrelevant and thus earn few marks.

When the question has been read and has been the subject of a little thought, the next step must be to plan the answer. At the very least this should take half a side of foolscap. The subject matter of each paragraph should be indicated: often this is most easily done by writing a series of rhetorical questions so that a given theme is developed step by step in an orderly and logical fashion. You will find that the class will object to this: they will say they have not enough time or that they know well enough what they wish to say. Point out to them that a well-planned, but concise essay, is a better essay than one which is long, detailed, but diffuse and incoherent. It will, of course, score more marks, but your aim is to teach them to write good essays: good marks will follow. If three-quarters of an hour is allowed for an answer not fewer than five and preferably as many as ten minutes should be insisted on for this vital job of planning the essay.

Two minor points may be mentioned in connection with the planning of the essay. You may like to use the analogy of the boy who takes part in a game of bridge or whist. What is his first action on being dealt a hand of cards? He picks them up, concealing them from his fellow players. Then he rearranges them in his hand in suits, noting the aces and possible tricks. When play begins, he aims to score as many tricks as possible and plays his cards accordingly. Far too many essay writers, in effect, pick up their cards, expose them carelessly and throw them down at random on the table, ignoring the strength or weaknesses of their hand. Such an analogy unfortunately presents the examiner as an 'opponent' and reintroduces the idea of the examination as a contest, but it is useful to a limited extent.

Your pupils should also be warned about the danger inherent in answers to questions which suggest the answer 'Yes' or 'No'.

Is the National Debt a burden on the community?

There is always a great temptation here to attempt to give an answer in the first paragraph – or even the first sentence – of an essay. This is especially true when the question takes the form of a quotation followed by the words 'Do you agree?' Having answered 'Yes' or 'No' as the case may be the candidate then proceeds to develop his theme and very often comes to quite the opposite conclusion in his final paragraph. Tell your class to imagine the sensation there would be in an assize court if Smith, accused of armed robbery, were brought before the judge, who, on hearing the charge, said, 'Guilty. Now let's hear the evidence.' Show your class how much more effective it would be to give both sides of the argument and to reserve judgment until the final paragraph.

Tell your class that to begin sentences with such phrases as 'It can thus easily be seen . . .' or 'It is therefore obvious . . .' is both unnecessary and bad style in writing. It is sometimes needlessly offensive, implying that if something is not obvious to a reader, then the reader and not the writer is to blame.

Some general points: accurate spelling and punctuation and correct grammatical usage are as necessary and desirable in the writing of essays in Economics as they are in any other subject; emphasise the need for clear, simple writing; the use of short sentences rather than long; the Anglo-Saxon word rather than the Latin. For all his brilliance as an economist, J. M. Keynes was deficient in this respect, preferring to coin unwieldy terms and outlandish jargon to describe relatively simple concepts. Had his 'General Theory' been as clearly written as his 'Economic Consequences of the Peace', its impact on statesmen and the public might have been more rapidly felt.

To summarise, the preparation of candidates for a particular examination by deliberate coaching or cramming tends to be sterile and unsatisfactory. The examiner is seen as an opponent or an enemy and teaching is orientated towards the aim of outwitting him, rather than towards developing the pupils' potentialities. Those qualities which the examiners hope to find in your candidate – a measure of accurate factual information, a knowledge of economic concepts, and an understanding of such concepts, together with the ability to analyse and discuss, to express opinions backed by sound argument – are the qualities which you as a teacher should try to develop as ends in themselves.

B. SPECIAL OR SCHOLARSHIP LEVEL ECONOMICS

We think that a different technique is required at this level. The scholarship candidate is a relatively simple problem, in the sense that it is stimulating to teach a pupil who wants to learn, who can, up to a point, teach himself and perhaps evoke ideas in your mind. We do not mean that he is simple because he is in fact endowed with a good mind, perhaps even an original mind. There is no reason why you should find this task embarassing. He is probably in his third year in the sixth, having already passed his 'A' level. He is certainly able, well above the average intellectual standard. The class is probably small in number, perhaps three or four, so that the tutorial method of discussion can be used very effectively. The scholarship-type paper, using the 'Oxbridge' examination as a criterion, is different from the usual 'A' level type of paper. The questions are usually more general and the candidate is expected to show good understanding and write clear, logical answers. Sometimes the questions are specialised but there is a very wide range of questions to choose from. Cambridge colleges set two papers, one of general questions covering Economics and Public Affairs, the other of more specific Economics questions. Oxford colleges set one paper with an equal number of questions on Economics and Politics. The candidate can select four questions concerned purely with Economics or Politics or general problems such as 'Was Mathematics invented or discovered?'. The aim of the paper is clearly to find out whether the candidate has the sort of mind capable of undertaking successfully the rigours of a university honours course. It is a more sophisticated approach, demanding wide reading, that is required. We think that the Socratic or Platonic method of teaching is best in which the teacher keeps the discussion going by asking provocative and, we hope, evocative questions addressed to each member of the class in turn preventing the talk from straying from the point and summing up every now and then, for instance, 'It seems to me then that Keynes said that rather than savings leading to investment, it was the other way round and investment would eventually bring savings into equilibrium with it. You take over now and tell us what happens next.' If the unfortunate student is baffled and stammers and stutters, unless one of his fellow victims dashes to his aid, you must do so, dropping a heavy hint.

It is a fruitful device to set a topic for the next period, such as the Economics of the Channel tunnel, give the class ideas where to find information, offer them a few suggestions of possible lines of approach such as 'Why will a tunnel be more economical than a bridge?', 'Should the project be managed by the British and French

Governments or by a private company at each end of the tunnel?', 'What are the likely economic consequences?', and so on? Set two pupils to prepare a paper on a topical problem like the transporting into and out of London daily of a large number of workers; one of them will be invited to read the paper, the other can perhaps expound on it a little and there can then be a discussion which the teacher must lead. Ask one of the class to state briefly what the problem is, why the City of London is inhabited by a mere five thousand caretakers and policemen at night but every morning half a million workers arrive from all quarters and eight hours later depart. Another can explain why London as a commercial and political centre has grown enormously, outside the boundaries of the original city. The two million or so people who work in London *must* travel at the same time and finish work more or less together because their business with each other is so intricately interwoven. Staggering hours becomes very difficult to work out with the result that there are peak hours and quiet periods on the railways and tubes and buses. Discuss the economic implications of the demand for seats in trains being so much greater than the supply, should British Rail raise the price of season tickets to the true economic level, using the power of the monopolist to exploit an inelastic demand? What about the motorists who drive into London head to tail, most cars containing only the driver? Few of them need to use their cars to carry on their business in London; they are driving purely because this mode of travel gives them greater utility. Should they be made to pay taxes at toll gates and high parking meter fees? You will find this kind of discussion can go on for several periods and you can bring out many fundamental economic principles. Incidentally, you should, with this group, try to get at least one double period a week in which to hold a really good, full discussion.

You cannot, of course, give answers to questions like 'Can we ever forgive the Chinese for inventing paper?'. Such questions are designed to test the candidate's wit and versatility, the elegance of his language, the originality of his mind, which are natural qualities. All you can do is to develop them. There is to help you do this an immense variety of journals published today. Encourage your pupils to read these. For example Unilever publish *Progress* and the big banks produce quarterly journals, as do other big firms like Hawker-Siddeley, which they are only too happy to send you regularly and

65

free. You might also join such societies like Hansard or the Institute of Public Administration. You should persuade the headmaster to allow the school to subscribe to the *Economist* and the boys can themselves buy papers like the *Economist* or *The Times* on favourable terms. A visit occasionally to a bookshop like the Economist Bookshop of the London School of Economics or Her Majesty's Stationery Office will repay you as you will be able to buy a wide variety of journals and paperbacks. You might join some of these societies yourself or subscribe to some of the journals. Your Inspector of Taxes will allow you reasonable expenditure of this kind as part of your professional equipment. If you do allow boys to borrow journals from the departmental library make sure you keep a record of these loans and insist strongly on all borrowed literature being returned. It is a good idea to cover journals either with brown paper or plastic to preserve them.

The Special level paper is a more difficult problem because it must be taken with the two 'A' level papers, all in the summer term. The boy who has done well at 'A' level the first time is naturally unwilling to go through the ordeal a second time. If he is going to take it at all he will do so when he takes 'A' level. In such a case he will need special lessons. The ordinary 'A' level teaching will not do. You should ask for five or six periods on your timetable for either a third-year sixth or Special level lessons. From experience we have found that if you have a third-year sixth who have come back to get a better grade in the January London G.C.E. they leave in the spring term, which leaves you free for your Special level teaching.

You must choose your candidates carefully partly because they are able and partly because they are willing to do the extra work. The first part of the paper, certainly as far as the London G.C.E. is concerned, demands an understanding of macro-economics. Let each member of the class explain with the aid of the blackboard the flow of goods and money between firms and households. Let them expound on the calculating of national income and expenditure; of gross national product, and the macro-equation. Show them how to distinguish clearly between two apparently conflicting statements like 'In order to invest more there must first be more savings', and 'In order to encourage more investment, there must first be more spending'. Have a period every now and then devoted to writing down impromptu answers to such questions; keep them practising until they are capable of setting down their thoughts succinctly and lucidly cutting out all the literary frills with which they bedeck their work. This is a most important exercise because sixth formers are inclined to be verbose. The effort to say something in a few well chosen words is an invaluable exercise in academic discipline which must help them in all their school work. We suggest that it is sometimes worthwhile encouraging a pupil or two who suffers from woolliness of thinking and literary expression to join this class, not with the intention of sitting the Special paper but in order to improve his academic work in general. In the bigger 'A' level class it is not easy to give individual attention to both the very good and the not so good without the run-of-the-mill average pupil becoming the victim of your good intentions. You must teach *all* the class to the best of your ability; the smaller Special paper class provides you with the opportunity to stretch your best pupils and to foster your stragglers, though happily at 'A' level these latter are few and far between.

The sort of short answer to be encouraged is something like this. The question asks if this statement is true or false: 'If the price of Good X rises, then demand for it will fall.' The answer is 'Yes, the statement is true if other things remain equal. If Mr Smith's income is unchanged he must decide whether to spend more on X in order to consume as much as before or spend as much and consume less or spend less on X and more on its substitute Y, the price of which has not risen. On the other hand if Mr Smith's income has also risen, then he will continue to demand as much X as before because he has more to spend and need not decrease his spending on other goods.'

Another question may take the form 'Write a short note on "The commercial banks have the unique function of creating credit in the United Kingdom" '. This statement is fundamentally true because firms who grant credit either to their customers or to each other in the end depend on a commercial bank giving credit to somebody in the form of an overdraft. The banks do not issue banknotes or mint coins, they merely permit a depositor to draw cheques for sums in excess of his credit or they extend the period of time in which an overdraft has to be paid back. So long as the flow of bank money in the form of cheques on current accounts goes on ceaselessly these cheques act as money in enabling people to demand effectively goods which otherwise they could not buy. The banks give credit to a manufacturer or to a finance house who in turn give credit to other manufacturers or to wholesalers and then to retailers who finally give credit to their customers the consumers.

C. ECONOMICS AS PART OF THE SIXTH-FORM COURSE

Most teachers of Economics are usually presented with a group of boys and told that this is their new 'A' level group. The combination of subjects which students are taking has been decided for a variety of reasons and may seem irrelevant except in so far as it affects the approach to teaching Economics because of the link with other subjects.

Nevertheless, we though it worthwhile at this point to give some considerations on Economics as part of a related group of subjects in the sixth form. These thoughts may be of value to teachers who advise boys in their sixth-form choices or to teachers who may be asked for their advice about introducing new subjects into the sixth-form curriculum.

In the science sixth subjects such as Chemistry, Physics, Biology and Maths overlap each other and support each other, employing a similar approach, the scientific approach. We expect those who wish to work at one of them to work at some of the others. A boy will not study Physics by itself if he has a serious academic intent. In the arts sixth it is the same with English, Foreign Languages, Art, History, etc. These subjects 'speak the same language' and share the same cultural ideas. So it should be too with those subjects which are all concerned with studying man acting out his life in society. These Social Science subjects, also, have much in common with each other. Economics overlaps with the human end of Geography, in such topics as population and location of industry. It overlaps with Government (or British Constitution) at an ever increasing number of points as the state moves inexorably into the economic field. Nowadays topics such as public finance and the public sector of industry are common to both. Economic History, in the hands of some historians, will provide the historical background to present-day descriptive Economics, and in the hands of a Marx or Rostow can be a springboard for fresh economic theorising. Economics,

Government, Economic History, Geography – these are all 'A' level subjects with most examining boards. They may be separate subjects or combined subjects, as with the Oxford and Cambridge Board's Economics and Political Studies. To these, new subjects are being added – Sociology (Oxford J.M.B.) and Business Studies (Cambridge).

When C. P. Snow came to rethink his famous dichotomy of the 'two cultures', he wrote a second edition to his essay to which he added the 'third culture' – the social sciences. And it was in the 'third culture' that he saw the hope of bridging the chasm between arts and science, a chasm he had previously been driven to consider as unbridgeable.

During the last twenty years the third culture has been growing at the universities faster than either of the other two. It is hardly too much to speak of a social science explosion. The influence of this explosion is now reaching down to the sixth forms in the schools, and more and more of them are adding either a full social science sixth to the more traditional arts and science sixths or, less drastically, adding one or two social science subjects to the sixth-form timetable. The cases of two schools illustrate what is happening. The first is a south London public school whose case was referred to in *The Times* (26 February 1968). Out of a sixth form of 198, 71 were on arts courses, 80 on the science side and 47 on the economics side. Only a few years ago the sixth form of this school consisted only of arts and science. The second case is a country grammar school in the north. Economics was introduced into this school as an Ordinary level subject in 1961 to be studied in the lower sixth. From 12 pupils who took the course three asked to take it to 'A' level in the following year. In 1963, 24 lower sixth pupils began studying for the 'A' level examination and a year later, when these had become the upper sixth, there were 45 pupils studying Economics to 'A' level. In that same year small groups of pupils began studying British Constitution, Economic History and Commerce at Ordinary level in the sixth form. We feel that there will be many more schools which can show a corresponding growth in Economics and associated subjects over a similar period of time. It is also important to point out that, in establishing themselves in schools, such courses have been able to take full benefit of the rapid increase in the number of sixth formers and have not had to poach pupils from other subjects.

If C. P. Snow was right in thinking that the social sciences are a bridge between the literate humanities and the numerate sciences, Economics is certainly the social science which stands closest to the scientific shore in that it is a subject which uses scientific techniques of analysis and study, and uses mathematical forms of expression whilst retaining a large element of literary material. Indeed, as Economics becomes increasingly mathematical we must consider including Mathematics as one of the subjects to be taken in the social science sixth, there now being little doubt that this course is the wise one to adopt for the boy who wishes to become an Economics specialist. The universities of Essex, Leeds, Lancaster and several others have shown a preference for those candidates for the Economics course who have already taken 'A' level Mathematics, and where many of the Business Studies degrees are concerned it is a faculty or departmental entrance requirement. So 'A' level Maths will need to be made available to those who need it by timetabling it against one of the other subjects.

However, there are many who will come to the social science sixth whose inclination or particular abilities will not lie in the direction of an 'A' level Mathematics course. These boys may be intending to take jobs after 'A' levels or they may be wanting to study Economics, not as specialists, but as part of a wider Social Science degree. For these, 'A' level Mathematics should certainly not be obligatory, though some minority-time Mathematics (perhaps the Additional Mathematics syllabus) or Statistics are very valuable additions to the course.

Social science sixths following the types of courses discussed above, have existed in some schools for the past thirty or forty years and have proved their worth by the generations of academics, bankers, industrialists, civil servants, journalists and, seemingly less likely, ministers of religion they have produced. Is such a form too specialised? The social science sixth is a specialist form, of course, in exactly the same way as the arts or science forms are and, not infrequently nowadays, we hear many arguments against such specialisation. But we would say this; in the hands of liberal-minded teachers who have the humility to realise their own small place in the cosmos, a full and liberal education can be followed within the framework of a course such as we have suggested. In his autobiography, C. S. Lewis tells how he was sent to work with an old schoolmaster who was to coach him for a classical scholarship. During those months under that old schoolmaster Lewis found that his whole outlook deepened and broadened in a way that went far beyond the classics. His whole attitude to life was affected. It was the teacher rather than the subject that mattered. Under a good teacher the Social Sciences provide as liberal an education as do any other branches of learning. Under a bad teacher any subject can be a mental straight-jacket.

It must be recognised, however, that specialisation in the sixth form, with its great academic advantages, is not without its dangers. There is always the danger, to which all specialists are exposed, that they may try to see the whole of life in terms of their own specialisation. Every subject has its own particular pitfalls. Economics is no different from the rest. In common with the natural sciences it is concerned with material things. There is always the danger that the eighteen-year-old, flushed with the sense of power that a little learning brings, may come to think that all life's problems can be answered in material and economic terms. After all, it is not uncommon for us to think we know all the answers at eighteen. The experienced schoolmaster will be aware of this danger and be on the lookout for it. He will not miss the chance to draw attention to the fact that, although the economic aspect of life is a very important aspect, it is by no means the only one. Many would hold that it is not the most important.

Economics will lie central in the social science group of subjects. Indeed, the form may be known as the Economics sixth and its teacher may find himself their form-master. If this is the case his concern for the pupils will be widened to take in their whole sixth-form development and future careers.

The number of subjects with which Economics can be linked in the sixth-form is large and seemingly grows larger each year as new subjects are introduced by the examining boards. We give below some of the possible combinations which the teacher of Economics is likely to encounter or may be obliged to consider starting, in the course of his sixth-form teaching. An attempt has been made to relate these courses to higher education and careers.

(a) *Economics, History, Geography.* An old faithful combination which is popular with pupils who have followed a traditional arts education in the lower school. Such a combination is becoming less

71

attractive to the universities, particularly if honours courses in Economics are intended, since the universities are showing a fondness for mathematical ability which this kind of sixth-form course often precludes. There is no reason why, however, this gap cannot be filled by providing Mathematics in the form suggested above. On the other hand this combination of subjects is useful for pupils intending to read joint honours courses say in Geography and Economics which are being developed in several of the new universities.

(b) *Economics, British Constitution, Geography or History.* A slightly more specialised course for pupils who would intend studying some politics in their degree, say P.P.E. at Oxford, or the London B.Sc.(Econ.). In place of History this group could include Latin or Greek, still regarded with affection at the older universities.

(c) *Economics, British Constitution, Economic History.* A group of subjects that are likely to have been studied by most teachers of Economics at some stage in their undergraduate careers. A good combination of subjects in that the head of department could work with specialist teachers who have interests and training similar to his own. Such a combination of subjects would form a firm foundation for any social science degree in Economics, Politics or Sociology. Referring to the last-named, it should be stressed that several examining boards have introduced a paper in Sociology which is bound to be of interest to many teachers.

(d) *Economics, Pure Mathematics with Statistics and an Arts subject.* The kind of course to encourage certain pupils to follow since many universities are looking more and more for potential undergraduates who have a good mathematical ability and who will become econometricians, statisticians, systems analysts, etc. We have commented above on the growing importance attached by universities to mathematical ability, particularly where courses involving Business Studies are concerned (Bath University of Technology makes potential undergraduates who have not got 'A' level Mathematics sit a special mathematical aptitude test before admitting them to their degree course). Moreover, this stressing of Mathematics has filtered down to the colleges of technology and commerce (the polytechnics designate), many of which have already established, or are in the process of establishing, degrees in Business Studies and Economics.

(e) *Economics, Mathematics and a science subject.* We are now moving away to some extent from our concept of a social science sixth, since in a combination such as this Economics is likely to occupy the role of the third subject. This kind of course would be useful to pupils intending to take a course of higher education in the applied sciences, particularly engineering. Several university degrees include Economics with applied sciences subjects, accepting the fact that the modern engineer is a person who should have management ability and should know subjects outside his own discipline.

(f) *Economics and Modern Languages.* Here again Economics will be the third subject but is relevant to a number of courses which universities and colleges are operating. Such courses stress the application of the language, rather that its literature, preparing students for careers in foreign marketing or the civil service. Most of these courses include a study of the Economics of the countries concerned and would offer to potential students an interesting break from traditional language-literature studies. Courses of this nature are operating at the Universities of Aston, Sussex and Surrey.

(g) *Economics, Art and a third subject.* Perhaps a seemingly odd combination of subjects at first but useful for pupils contemplating careers in architecture or town and country planning.

We apologise if our emphasis has been towards university courses. It is not the sole purpose of schools to prepare pupils for university entrance, nor is it our duty to give courses specifically related to intended careers. However, given the proliferation of a large number of new courses at universities which include Economics we feel that some of the above combinations might be noted and brought to the attention of your pupils. As regards specific careers the use of Economics within a social science course is invaluable to those entering professions such as banking, accountancy, the law, surveying of many kinds, estate management and many careers in public services and local government.

5

OBJECTIVE TESTING

Subjective and objective testing

The teaching of Economics, as does the teaching of most other subjects, poses the continuous problem of assessing pupils' understanding of the ideas which together make up the basis of the subject. Assessment or testing may be carried out either subjectively or objectively: subjectively by the well-tried method of essay writing, where the pupils' efforts are assessed by the teacher or examiner; or objectively, through specially designed questions or groups of questions which have a single correct answer. In this case assessment of the result bears solely upon the questions and does not depend upon the subjective factors which are present when the examinee writes an essay which is read and marked by the examiner.

The weekly essay has much in its favour and, in no way, do we suggest that it should be replaced by objective testing methods. The essay is a useful way of getting pupils to read more widely; it is an exercise for the pupils in collating and expressing the ideas they have absorbed from their teachers, their textbooks and the articles they have read; it serves as practice designed to make them familiar with the techniques they will need to use when sitting a public examination; and the essay forms a useful adjunct to revision work as the examination approaches. The efficacy of the essay as a test of the understanding of economic ideas, however, is obscured by the degree to which any pupil has mastered or has failed to master the complex techniques required to produce a coherent piece of work that we call an essay.

The purposes of objective testing

Much work is presently being carried out on how continuous testing can be undertaken throughout the pupil's sixth-form career and on how that testing may reinforce the pupil's understanding and learning. At the same time at least one examining board will introduce objective questions into the 'A' level papers in Economics in 1971,

74

whilst another board has been experimenting in and using this type of question in 'A' level General Studies papers for several years. The reason for this chapter therefore is twofold; it appears because it seems to us that a review of objective testing techniques will be helpful to the Economics teacher who is anxious to discover an efficient method of testing his pupils' economic understanding, as well as to the teacher whose pupils may well soon be faced with this type of questioning technique in their 'A' level examinations. The technique of objective testing most likely to be used by the examining boards is that using multiple choice questions. One of the two papers will be devised so that it contains perhaps seventy-five questions, each of which will have a choice of five answers, one of which is the correct answer, the other four wrong answers being termed 'distractors'. Other types of objective questions which may be used include multiple completion questions, assertion reason questions, 'true' or 'false' questions and structured questions.

The purpose of objective question papers is to eliminate the element of chance in the present type of paper in which a good candidate on a bad day will fail and a bad candidate on a good day will pass, or in which the value judgments of an examiner vary from day to day or from script to script. Proponents of this type of test maintain that it is almost foolproof. If candidates understand Economics they will be able to reason why four statements out of five are false or true; therefore the fifth is the answer. It seems unlikely that the examining boards will allow teachers to retain question papers. On the other hand teachers will clearly wish to give their pupils tests. Later in the chapter we therefore give examples of these types of questions for guidance.

Members of the committee have been using objective questions with their pupils in the last two or three years, more to test the questions than to test the pupils, and indeed in using objective questions the pre-testing of the questions is important when those questions are to be used for examination purposes. Pupils reactions to these questions vary but generally they manage to complete the questions in the allotted time. They sometimes dislike not being able to write down the reasons why they made a particular choice and they find it a tiring experience. For teachers, little or no significant change in their teaching methods is necessary but they should give their pupils practice in tackling this type of paper. It will

75

probably be necessary to pay a little more attention to going through the fundamental processes of economic activity with great care until the pupils are familiar with them and understand clearly the connections between the different stages of a process and between the process and other sequences of economic events. The danger in studying Economics is that pupils, at least in the early stage try to learn by rote, whereas they must be persuaded to understand so that when dealing with an objective type of question they can eliminate quickly through logical thinking what is wrong. They must acquire the apparatus of thinking that Keynes postulated Economics to be about.

Apart from their importance as examination questions, the various types of objective questions can be extremely useful to the teacher because not only do they test understanding they also reinforce it. The teaching of many subjects, and Economics is among them, to an examination syllabus imposed by an outside body such as an examining board tends to become rigid. The pupil tends to feel that he must memorise facts and his subject is presented to him under the stress of examination requirements in a way which, all too frequently, encourages this inflexibility. What we really want to encourage in our pupils is a lively curiosity, a depth of understanding and an ability to apply ideas and theories to the solution of specific problems. Objective testing techniques go beyond the simple ability to recall and reinforce the understanding of the pupils, becoming an important teaching aid as well as a method of testing. Multiple choice questions are especially useful for pin-pointing topics where additional revision and study are required, but perhaps the most useful are structured questions of the type to be found in the many workbooks currently available. Many of these workbooks are directly related to a textbook and the two are meant to be used together. The questions in the workbook are worked out in close conjunction with the relevant chapter in the textbook. The structured questions require answers to several parts, the answer to the second part being based upon the deductions made to provide the answer to the first part. Thus, each question can be designed or structured to test basic understanding of a concept and then to test the pupils' ability to apply the concept to a specific problem and arrive at a reasoned solution.

Professor Nevin's *Workbook of Economic Analysis* published by

Macmillan as a companion to his *Textbook of Economic Analysis*, illustrates this technique particularly well. This book should be assessed in the light of the declared aim of the author, set out in the foreword. He states the modest aim of reducing the 'grubbing around for real life data on which analytical techniques can be tried'. He stresses that the manipulation of numerical data is not the only useful form of training for the economist nor does he consider that only quantitative Economics is important. In section one of the *Workbook* there are ten questions each with two parts on the topic of individual demand. The pupil must first understand how to construct indifference curves and the price opportunity line. He is then asked to work out points of consumer equilibrium and substitution, price and income effects. Finally he is asked to assess the relative strengths of the various effects. The usefulness of such exercises lies in the structured or logical build-up of the questions. When the pupil has studied chapter 3 of Nevin's *Textbook* and completed the numerical questions in section one of the *Workbook* he will not only understand the mechanism by which economists analyse individual consumer behaviour but he will have had experience in dealing with the numerous facets of handling the several variables involved in the problems of consumer choice. The method of solving numerical problems will help the pupil to approach the problems of analysis and application logically and, at the end of the day, although he may not be able to repeat by heart the Law of Equi-marginal Returns or the Principle of Substitution he will have a good understanding of consumer behaviour, including that which is probably most difficult for the new pupil to understand, the interrelationships between income, substitution and price effects. Moreover, he is fully prepared to go one stage further and examine the concept of elasticities of demand in relation to the problem of consumer behaviour, rather than as an isolated topic. The advantage of such an approach is clear. The young pupil meeting the subject for the first time, frequently in his lower sixth-form year, tends to place each of the Economics topics in a separate mental pigeon-hole and this tendency more than anything prevents his understanding of the interrelationships of economic ideas.

In terms of objective testing the two types of question discussed, namely multiple choice and structured questions, represent opposite ends of the same scale. The other types of question which may be

77

used are variations on either of these two basic types. The assertion-reason question is similar to the structured question whilst the multiple completion and true or false types are variations of the multiple choice question. Good examples of most of the different types of objective questions can be found in a very useful booklet by G. F. Stanlake called *Objective Tests in Economics* published by Longman. Nevin's *Workbook of Economic Analysis* is published by Macmillan. The latter book not only contains the structured questions noted above but also a good selection of multiple choice questions.

In the study of the various divisions of Economics so much depends for the understanding of the more advanced ideas upon the perfection of understanding of the fundamental ideas that failure to understand from the beginning creates severe difficulties for the pupil at a more advanced stage. For this reason objective testing either through the use of the various workbooks available or through regular tests devised by the teacher will not only reinforce the pupils' understanding of Economics but will also help the teacher to estimate the degree to which his pupils have understood the economic ideas he puts before them. He will be able to pinpoint the areas of knowledge where understanding is less than perfect.

The techniques of testing

The use of objective tests emphasises the teacher's interest in his pupil's understanding and, in fact, objective tests assess whether the subject is understood. For instance, one of the sample questions (question 39) contained in the multiple choice section refers to gross domestic product. If the pupil understands that imports cannot possibly be a part of the domestic product he will naturally deduct the total of imports from his total. If he appreciates that indirect taxes on consumer expenditure raise prices above factor costs and to include them would give a false picture of the domestic product he will logically deduct taxes. On the other hand, because subsidies tend to bring prices down to an unreal level he will add them to his total. If he genuinely understands this he will be able to answer the question in a few moments.

The achievement of understanding depends upon the pupil exercising certain abilities and in testing understanding the teacher is testing or measuring these abilities. The abilities capable of being measured by objective questions may be listed as: the ability to gain knowledge of the facts and theories of the subject and of the general and specific methods of analysis employed; the ability to comprehend the facts, theories and methods of analysis; the ability to apply the theories and analytical methods to real or imagined situations; the ability to evaluate and investigate the relative importance of the facts and theories; and the ability to use terminology and conventions correctly, to organise and present ideas and statements in a clear and logical form.

In testing and measuring these abilities the teacher will gain a good idea of how well his pupils understand the subject. Moreover, the use of objective tests will demand that pupils exercise these abilities and in so doing they will reinforce their understanding and learning of the subject.

There are already several books which provide ready-made sets of objective questions but teachers may well wish to devise their own 'bank' of questions. In devising a series of questions the teacher will first of all need to decide upon both the subject matter and the pupils' abilities to be tested. When writing multiple choice questions the technique is to write both the question and the answers to the question together. Only one of the answers must be correct and care must be exercised that neither the question nor the answers contain ambiguities. The 'distractors' or wrong answers must not be possible answers to the question but they should be fairly close to the correct answer. For instance the distractors could be statements of fairly common mistakes that pupils make. If the teacher aims to build up a 'bank' of questions then it is important that these questions are pre-tested from two points of view; first to determine whether the question produces the correct answer and secondly to see whether the correct answer was obtained by the exercise of those abilities that the question was designed to test. One way of pre-testing questions is to present the questions to the class and when they have completed them to ask a member of the class to state his answer and to outline on the blackboard how he arrived at his answer. The class will gain experience in handling the questions and the teacher will discover whether the abilities the question was designed to test have indeed been tested.

In designing a complete test, whether it is comprised of twenty

79

or a hundred questions, a further problem the teacher will have to solve is that of the 'weighting' to be given to the different abilities being tested. How much emphasis is given to the pupil's ability to gain knowledge as opposed to his ability to apply a learned theory to a given problem will depend upon many factors such as the age of the pupil and the extent of his experience in the study of Economics. With a pre- 'O' level class the emphasis will usually be on the pupil's knowledge and in a test the weighting of abilities will be of the order of 40 % of the marks allotted for knowledge, 30 % for comprehension, 20 % for application, and 10 % for evaluation and investigation. At higher levels, in the sixth form, much greater emphasis will be laid on comprehension and application and accordingly far fewer marks will be allotted for knowledge.

Examples of questions

In this final section we include a selection of objective questions. Most of the examples are of the type known as multiple choice questions because this is the type of question most popularly used for classroom testing and because it is the type that the examining boards are most likely to use. A few examples of structured questions are included but we have restricted their number because a much better idea of the techniques of devising structured questions can be gained from the growing numbers of workbooks that are available than we could hope to present here. In the case of the multiple choice questions the correct answer is indicated by an asterisk. It must be noted that the questions that follow are of varying standards for different age groups or abilities – they are not intended solely to meet the requirements of 'A' level or 'O' level examinations. These test questions are intended simply as examples of the types which may be used. They have not been subjected to the rigorous screening to which the examining boards would put their examination questions.

A. Structured Questions

QUESTION 1

The diagram shows the consumption pattern of the individual consumer for goods *X* and *Y*. *AB* is the consumer's price opportunity line when Good *X* costs 15p. per lb and Good *Y* costs 20p. per lb.

OBJECTIVE TESTING

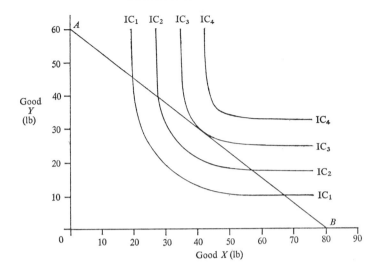

With respect to this information:
(a) Estimate the consumer's weekly income.
(b) Mark on the diagram the point of consumer equilibrium.
(c) When in equilibrium, how much of X and Y will he buy?
(d) On the diagram illustrate the effect of a rise in the price of X of 5p. per lb.
(e) On the diagram illustrate the effect of a fall of £2 per week in consumer's income.
(f) How much of X and Y respectively will he now buy as a result of the fall in income?

QUESTION 2

On the graph paper provided construct supply and demand schedules for the product S from the data given:

Price per ton (£)	Quantity demanded (000 tons)	Quantity supplied (000 tons)
0·50	41	6
1·00	32	14
1·50	24	21
2·00	19	27
2·50	15	32
3·00	11	35
3·50	8	37

(a) What is the equilibrium price and quantity for product S?
(i) price
(ii) quantity

81

(b) What formula would you use to determine the price elasticity of demand for a product?

(c) From the data estimate the price elasticity of demand for product *S* if the price increases from £1 to £1·05 per ton.

(d) Is the price elasticity of demand for product *S* at a price of £1 per ton:
 (i) relatively elastic
 (ii) relatively inelastic
 (iii) equal to unity?

QUESTION 3

The diagram shows the position of the cost curves (total costs per unit of output (ATC), average variable costs (AVC) and marginal costs (MC)) of a firm operating under conditions of perfect competition in the short run.

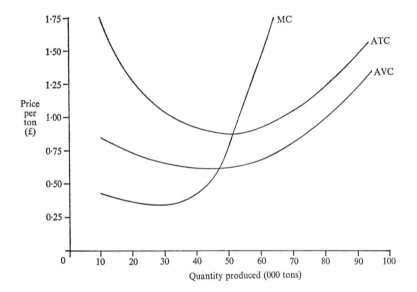

On the diagram:
(a) Indicate by the letters *SS* the extent of the short run supply curve of the firm.
(b) Draw in the approximate position of the average fixed cost curve (AFC).
On the question sheet:
(c) State how many tons the firm would produce, in the short run, if the selling price were fixed at:
 (i) £0·50 per ton
 (ii) £0·85 per ton
 (iii) £1·50 per ton
(d) At what selling price would the firm produce its optimum output?

82

OBJECTIVE TESTING

The following diagram shows the average and marginal costs and the average and marginal revenue of a firm with a monopoly in the production of a particular article.

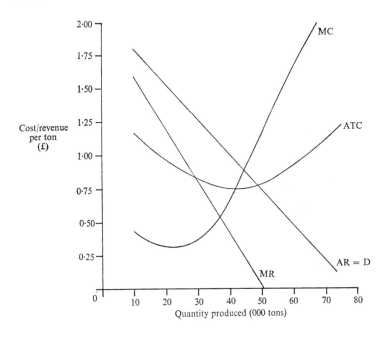

Under these conditions:
(a) How much will the monopolist produce?
(b) What price will he charge?
On the diagram:
(c) Illustrate a fall in demand for the monopolist's product and show how this fall would affect price and output.
(d) At the new demand shade in the area indicating the monopolist's profit.

QUESTION 5

(a) The U.K. balance of payments for 1967 in £ million was:

Current Account

Visible trade	Imports	5,673
	Exports	5,023
	Visible balance	650

Is the balance plus or minus?   Answer: minus

83

Invisibles	Government expenditure		-449
	Other invisibles		$+585$
	Invisible balance		$+136$

What is the current balance of visible trade and invisibles?

Answer: -514

Name three invisible items.

(b) *Long-term Capital Account*

Official investment	(net)	-54
Private investment	(net)	$+28$
Balance of long-term capital		-26

What is the balance of current and long-term capital transactions, i.e. the basic balance?

Answer: -540

(c) Monetary movements in 1967 were:

Exchange adjustments	-101
Miscellaneous capital	$+70$
Changes in liabilities of non-sterling currencies	$+193$
Changes in external liabilities in sterling	$+288$
Changes in account with I.M.F.	-318
Transfers to dollar reserves	$+204$
Changes in gold reserves	$+16$
Balance of monetary movements	$+320$

What is the balancing item?

Answer: $X(+220)$

X This is the difference between the basic balance and the balance of monetary movements.

B. Multiple Choice Questions

1. In a money-using capitalist society the economic problem of 'what goods' shall be produced is solved primarily by:
   (a) people advertising their wants
   (b) direction by the government
   *(c) the pattern of consumers' spending
   (d) people producing directly to satisfy their own wants

2. What economic principle or law does the following formula illustrate:

$$\frac{M.U.a}{P.a} = \frac{M.U.b}{P.b} = \frac{M.U.c}{P.c} = \frac{M.U. \ldots r}{P. \ldots r}$$

(where $M.U.$ is marginal utility, $P.$ is price and $a,b,c \ldots r$ are various goods bought by an individual consumer.)
   (a) Diminishing marginal utility
   *(b) The Law of Equimarginal Returns
   (c) Say's Law of Markets

(d) The Principle of Substitution

3. If $\dfrac{M.U.a}{P.a} > \dfrac{M.U.b}{P.b} = \dfrac{M.U.c}{P.c}$ etc.

What action will the individual consumer take to attain an equilibrium position?
   (a) Stop buying a
   (b) Buy more of b and c and less of a
   *(c) Buy more of a and less of b and c
   (d) Take no action

4. In the typical demand schedule, quantity demanded:
   (a) varies directly with price
   (b) varies proportionately with price
   *(c) varies inversely with price
   (d) is independent of price

5. The demand curve for a good slopes:
   (a) downwards from right to left in perfect competition
   (b) upwards from left to right if demand is inelastic
   *(c) downwards from left to right if demand is relatively elastic
   (d) downwards from left to right if demand is perfectly inelastic
   (e) downwards vertically if demand is perfectly elastic
   Which of these statements is true?

6. If tape recorders suddenly become more popular than record players, which of the following consequences will happen?
   *(a) A shortage of tape recorders
   (b) A shortage of record players
   (c) A surplus of tape recorders
   (d) Higher production of record players
   (e) A fall in the price of tape recorders

7. Elasticity of demand:
   (a) measures changes in the quantity of a good consumed caused by changes in supply
   (b) reflects changes in the tastes and preferences of consumers at different times
   *(c) is the responsiveness of demand to changes in price related to the number of substitutes there are for a good and to the income of the consumer at that time
   (d) depends on whether a good is a necessity to life or a luxury
   (e) is the seasonal variation of demand for a good such as coal, the demand rises in winter and falls in summer
   Only one of the above statements is an accurate definition of elasticity of demand; which one is it?

The first diagram overleaf applies to questions 8–10. It shows supply curves at different periods of time, 1 and 2.

8. The curve S_1 shows that:
   (a) more X is put on the market as the price falls
   (b) as less of X is supplied to the market, the price falls
   *(c) more X is put on the market as the price rises
   (d) supply is independent of price

Price of X ($£1$ unit)

Quantity of X supplied

9. The movement of the curve from S_1 to S_2 shows:
   *(a) a decrease of supply at all relevant prices
   (b) a contraction of supply
   (c) supply greater in period 2 than in period 1
   (d) a condition of inelastic supply

10. The shift of the curve from S_1 to S_2 could be caused by:
    (a) a government subsidy to producers of X
    *(b) an increase in the wage rates paid to workers in industry X
    (c) improved techniques of production in X
    (d) a fall in the price of raw materials used in manufacturing X

11. If there is a large find of gas in the North Sea which of the following consequences will happen in the long run?
    (a) A scarcity of gas
    (b) A rise in the price of oil
    (c) A rise in the price of gas
    *(d) A fall in the price of gas
    (e) A scarcity of oil

12. The Theory of Diminishing Marginal Returns states that:
    (a) every increase in output will produce a diminishing amount of revenue
    (b) as output increases, price must fall, therefore returns will fall
    (c) each additional expansion of output will cost more to produce and so result in a fall in returns
    (d) as a firm grows larger, so will its productivity diminish
    *(e) each successive application of labour and capital to a given area of land will eventually, other things being equal, yield a less than proportionate increase in output
    Only one of the above statements is completely true; which one is it?

13.

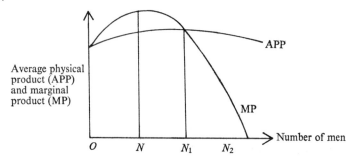

Average physical product (APP) and marginal product (MP)

APP

MP

Number of men

O N N_1 N_2

At what output on the above diagram do diminishing returns set in?
*(a) ON
(b) ON_1
(c) ON_2
(d) the output is now shown on the diagram

14. Marginal cost is:
    (a) the lowest cost of producing a good incurred by a firm
    (b) the cost of production of the most inefficient firm in an industry
    (c) the cost of production of the most efficient firm in an industry
    *(d) the cost of production of the last or extra unit of a good produced by a firm
    (e) the cost of production at which the minimum profit is obtained by a firm
    Which of the above statements is true?

15. A firm in perfect competition will expand output to the point at which:
    *(a) marginal cost is equal to marginal revenue
    (b) price is equal to the price at which all other firms in the market are selling
    (c) average cost is equal to average revenue
    (d) marginal profit is at the maximum rate that is total revenue is greater than total cost at this output than at any other output
    (e) supply is equal to demand
    Only one of these statements is exactly true; which one is it?

16. The original theory of economic rent was propounded by: (a) Adam Smith (b) Thomas Malthus *(c) David Ricardo (d) Stanley Jevons (e) Alfred Marshall

17. Economic rent is:
    (a) the transfer value of a factor of production from one kind of employment to another
    (b) the rent of a house which is determined by supply and demand in a free market
    *(c) the excess earning of a factor of production above its opportunity cost
    (d) the rent at which the owner of property either a house or land thinks it just worthwhile to let his property
    (e) the rent of a factor that is governed by its scarcity in relation to the demand for it
    All the above statements have some measure of truth in them; which do you think is the most accurate definition?

18. That part of the earnings of a factor of production over and above the payment required to keep the factor in its present employment is:
    (a) transfer earnings
    *(b) economic rent
    (c) opportunity costs
    (d) marginal costs
    (e) comparative costs

19. The rate of interest is:
    (a) the price of money at which the marginal efficiency of capital and liquidity preference are equal
    (b) the measure of the element of risk in the lending or borrowing of money
    (c) the lender's valuation of the loss of liquidity over a period of time

*(d) the borrower's expectation of profit

(e) the current bank rate

Four of these statements are wholly or substantially true, one is largely untrue, which one is that?

20. The following are possible actions which could be taken by the Bank of England:
    (a) Buy stock on the open market
    (b) Lower bank rate
    (c) Call for 'special deposits'
    (d) Increase funding of the National Debt

    Which of the above actions would be consistent with a 'dear' money policy?
      (i) (a), (c) and (d)
    * (ii) (c) and (d)
      (iii) (a) and (c)
      (iv) (a) and (d)

21. A cheque is:
    (a) a promissory note issued by a commercial bank
    (b) legal tender money
    (c) an order on the post office to pay a sum of money to the person named on the cheque
    (d) a bill of exchange between the buyer and seller of a good
    *(e) an instruction to a commercial bank to pay a stated sum of money to the person named on the cheque by the writer of the cheque who has a current account at the bank

    Which of the above statements is true?

22. A discount house is:
    (a) a store which gives discount to account customers
    (b) a merchant bank which accepts bills of exchange
    (c) a commercial bank which discounts treasury bills
    *(d) a specialist finance company which lends money by discounting bills of exchange or treasury bills
    (e) a firm of stockbrokers who buy or sell securities at a discount

    One of these statements is true. Which is it?

23. Which of the following is the most accurate description of the big three commercial banks in England, i.e. Barclays, Lloyds, National Provincial/Westminster?
    (a) Monopoly
    (b) Monopsony
    *(c) Oligopoly
    (d) Monopolistic competition
    (e) Imperfect competition

24. The assets of the English commercial banks consist of:
    (a) cash in hand and at Bank of England
    (b) money at call
    (c) treasury and other bills of exchange
    (d) investments
    (e) advances

Which is the most liquid asset?	Answer: (a)
Which is probably the most profitable asset?	Answer: (e)
Which form the liquidity ratio?	Answer: (a), (b), (c)

OBJECTIVE TESTING

25. The proportion of their total assets which banks keep in liquid form is:
    (a) 40%
    *(b) 28%
    (c) 8%
    (d) 15%

26. Which of the following interest rates are not directly linked with bank rate?
    (a) Rates on loans by commercial banks
    (b) Rates on deposit accounts with commercial banks
    (c) Rates given by unit trusts
    (d) Rates charged by building societies
    (e) Market rate for treasury bills
    Are they?
    (i) (a), (b) and (c)
    (ii) (b), (c) and (d)
    *(iii) (c) and (d)
    (iv) (d) and (e)
    (v) (c), (d) and (e)

27. The average income per head per annum in the United Kingdom is £600 and in Malaysia is £30. It does not follow that a person in the U.K. is 20 times better off than one in Malaysia for two of the following reasons; which are they?
    (a) The population of Malaysia is 10 times larger than that of the U.K.
    (b) The U.K. currency is based on the pound and the Malaysia on the ducat.
    *(c) Far more transactions in Malaysia take place without the use of money.
    (d) Expectation of life in Malaysia is half that in the U.K.
    *(e) Cost of living in the U.K. is much higher than in Malaysia.

28. Which of the following is the Fisher Formula?
    (a) $Y = C+I+G$
    (b) $\epsilon = \dfrac{p \triangle x}{x \triangle p}$
    *(c) $MV = PT$
    (d) $k = \dfrac{1}{1 - MPC}$

29. Which of the following taxes is progressive?
    *(a) Surtax
    (b) Selective employment tax
    (c) Corporation tax
    (d) Purchase tax
    (e) Capital gains tax

30. Which of the following statements is correct?
    A regressive tax:
    (a) is one that diminishes as income rises thus yielding less revenue
    (b) is one that rises as income increases
    (c) is one that falls as income diminishes
    *(d) is one that is related to the value of a good or service consumed by the taxpayer regardless of his income
    (e) is one that yields less revenue to the government because it tends to decrease demand for the good or service taxed

D

31. Which of the following taxes are regressive?
    (a) Income tax
    (b) Surtax
    (c) Death duties
    (d) Excise duties
    (e) Customs duties
    Are they:
      (i) (a), (b) and (d)
      (ii) (a), (b) and (e)
      (iii) (b), (c) and (d)
      (iv) (c), (d) and (e)
    *(v) (d) and (e)

32. Which one of the following firms pays income tax and surtax?
    *(a) A partnership
    (b) A private limited company
    (c) A public joint-stock company
    (d) A holding company
    (e) A co-operative society

33. Which three of the following items in the Balance of Payments Account are invisibles?
    (a) Imports of goods
    (b) Aviation
    (c) Tourism
    (d) Private investment overseas
    (e) Government expenditure overseas
Are they:
      (i) (a), (b) and (c)
      (ii) (b), (c) and (d)
    *(iii) (b), (c) and (e)
      (iv) (c), (d) and (e)
      (v) (b), (d) and (e)

34. The International Monetary Fund was established to perform one of the following functions; which one is it?
    (a) To lend money to an underdeveloped country to create capital goods
    (b) To help a country to balance her domestic budget
    (c) To help a country to rectify a chronic imbalance in her economy
    *(d) To enable a country to make good a deficit in her annual balance of payments by means of a loan of gold or foreign exchange
    (e) To lend a country money in order to build up her defence forces

35. If exports from the U.K. to the U.S.A. fall and imports from the U.S.A. to the U.K. rise, one of the following things will happen, other things being equal:
    (a) The exchange value of the pound will rise
    (b) The exchange value of the dollar will fall
    (c) The price of U.K. exports to the U.S.A. will rise
    *(d) The exchange value of the pound will fall
    (e) Gold will flow from the U.S.A. to the U.K.
    Which is it?

36. A government will devalue its currency if:
    (a) there is a chronic balance of payments deficit

*(b) if exports are greater than imports
(c) if the terms of trade are persistently adverse
(d) if imports are rising faster than exports
(e) if there is a steady outflow of gold to foreign countries
Which of these factors would not lead to devaluation?

37. The following figures show demand elasticities for a country's exports abroad and its own demand elasticities for imports. Which set offers the best prospects, for a successful devaluation?
    *(a) exports 0·9, imports 1·0
    (b) exports 2·5, imports 1·6
    (c) exports 2·0, imports 0·7
    (d) exports 1·5, imports 1·8

38. If a country devalues its currency, one of the following consequences will follow:
    (a) the price of exports will rise
    (b) the price of imports will fall
    (c) the price level at home will fall
    *(d) the price of exports will fall to foreigners
    (e) the standard of living at home will rise

39. Given the following data from the 1966 National Income and Expenditure Estimates, what was the gross domestic product at factor cost?

	£ million
Consumers' expenditure	24,000
Public authorities' expenditure	7,000
Gross fixed investment	6,000
Capital investment	200
Exports of goods and services	7,000
Total final expenditure on goods and services	44,200
Imports of goods and services	7,000
Taxes on expenditure	6,000
Subsidies	600

Was it:
    (a) £43,800 million
    (b) £42,600 million
    *(c) £31,800 million
    (d) £31,200 million

40. If the marginal propensity to consume in an economy is 0·8, an expenditure of £200 million on a schools building project would raise national income by a further:
    *(a) £800 million
    (b) £200 million
    (c) £1,600 million
    (d) £500 million

41. Which one of the following distinguished economists is usually associated most closely with the theory of the multiplier:
    (a) Alfred Marshall
    *(b) John Maynard Keynes
    (c) A. C. Pigou

(d) R. G. Lipsey
(e) Lord (Lionel) Robbins

42. The theory of the multiplier states that:
   (a) the larger the firm the greater will its productivity be in proportion to the quantity of factors of production employed
   (b) the marginal propensity to save will increase disproportionally to the rate of increase of income
   *(c) each act of NEW investment will create further spending and saving until the NEW income created will be equal to the original investment multiplied by the multiplier
   (d) each additional act of investment will create a more than proportional amount of new income equal to the marginal propensity to consume
   (e) each increase of national income will result in an increase in the propensity to consume and thus to a rise in aggregate supply and aggregate demand
   Four of the above statements are false, which one is true?

43. There is an increase in investment in an economy of £1,000 and the marginal propensity to consume is $\frac{4}{5}$. By how much will total income increase?
   (a) £1,000
   (b) £4,000
   *(c) £5,000
   (d) £200
   (e) £800

44. If the marginal propensity to save is $\frac{1}{5}$, and the marginal propensity to tax is $\frac{1}{5}$, and the marginal propensity to import is $\frac{1}{10}$, what would be the size of the multiplier?
   (a) 5
   (b) 10
   *(c) 2
   (d) 3

45. Which one of the following policies is the government very unlikely to follow if there is a serious inflation?
   (a) Raise bank rate
   (b) Impose a wages and prices squeeze
   *(c) Increase imports and decrease exports
   (d) Decrease imports and increase exports
   (e) Raise income tax in order to discourage consumer spending

46. If there is inflation a government will take some of the following measures:
   (a) Raise bank rate
   (b) Restrict rises in wages
   (c) Request commercial banks to lend less
   (d) Reduce the rate of income tax
   (e) Lower tariffs on imports
   Are they:
   (i) (a) and (d)
   (ii) (c), (d) and (e)
   *(iii) (a), (b) and (c)
   (iv) (c) and (d)
   (v) (b) and (c)

6

MATHEMATICS IN ECONOMICS

One of the most important developments in the study of Economics in recent decades has been the increasing use of Mathematics in order to give greater precision to existing theories and to test them fully. Besides this we have seen an increasing use of statistics and the quantification of certain concepts such as the size and rate of growth of the national income. The mathematical presentation of theories is now well established in universities but we are aware of the fact that many teachers of Economics in secondary schools have a certain mistrust of this tool, perhaps because of a feeling that they are coping perfectly satisfactorily with a verbal presentation and see no need for an alternative which appears to them only to complicate.

To the economist Mathematics is a tool. It is not a substitute for economic ideas – it is a precise form of presenting some of them and in this role is becoming increasingly used among professional economists and university teachers. We do not intend mathematical jargon to be used as a smoke screen with which to cover a mental landscape devoid of ideas or knowledge. We hope that use of mathematical presentations at elementary level will help us to amplify, to unify and to generalise on points of economic theory which we wish to teach. The mathematics itself is not intended as another academic exercise, nor are we advocating the mathematical approach in place of the verbal approach. The latter must be taught. Any pupil can memorise $MV = PT$ and say 'this is the Quantity Theory'. He must be able to state what the letters mean and explain the theory in detail, together with its weaknesses. Similarly elasticity of demand can be written as:

$$\varepsilon_D = \frac{p\Delta x}{x\Delta p}$$

but this formula only tells us how to calculate elasticity. It does not explain what the concept is, namely the responsiveness of demand to small changes in price, but, however much we favour the verbal approach we must admit that it has some weaknesses, perhaps the main one being a vagueness, a certain ambiguity in some cases. For

93

instance, one teacher may find that the Theory of Value as explained in terms of diminishing marginal utility is a difficult concept to grasp because of its vagueness as a consequence of which he finds it difficult to put over to his class. A number of abstract concepts are involved – the margin, the psychological barrier which cuts off worthwhile from non-worthwhile purchases – diminishing utility and the distinction between total and marginal utility. Was it not because of this vagueness that the marginal preferences theory and the use of indifference curves were adopted as alternatives and therefore more precise presentations of the Theory of Value?

With more complex topics of economic theory the case for a mathematical presentation becomes even stronger. For example the problem of economic growth needs to be discussed in the light of growth models such as the Harrod/Domar one. It is possible to present this mathematically, as is done in a simple way in Stonier and Hague, *Textbook of Economic Theory*, chapter xxvi, pp. 513–29. It is also possible to give a mainly verbal presentation, as is done in Jan Pen, *Modern Economics*, chapter x, pp. 189–201, although even here some equations are included. We suggest that this problem could be discussed using both methods, with your scholarship sixth or with your 'A' level group.

Professor R. G. Lipsey has argued in the journal of the Economics Association (Spring 1964, vol. 5, pt. 3) that the days of the B.Sc. (Econ.) graduate who knows no Mathematics are limited, but may last another ten years and he issues the following warning. 'If you have any intention of going on to become an academic economist for goodness' sake learn Mathematics now. If you do not, you will, like myself, regret it for the rest of your career as a research economist.' We know that we are not training research economists, but we are training social scientists, and if they are to be truly scientific we feel that they should have at their disposal the tools of the scientists, the most important of which is Mathematics and the next most important a familiarity with statistics.

As teachers of Economics we regard ourselves as social scientists and pride ourselves on having a scientific approach to our subject. We take a situation and analyse it with the tools we have at our disposal. Let us take a simple example, the sort of exercise we would be likely to set to our class as an application of theories already taught, and see what tools we can use in solving it.

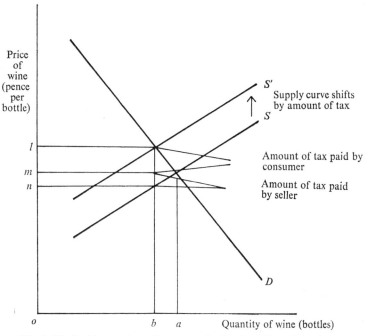

Fig. 1. The incidence of taxation: example showing effect of a sales tax.

The Government proposes to introduce a tax on, let us say, wine. How effective will this tax be in earning revenue for the state, and in taking purchasing power out of the public's pocket (we imply that every tax today has an aspect of fiscal policy in it and is not purely for revenue-raising purposes)? How much of this tax will be paid by the consumer and how much of it by the seller? We are probably familiar with the elementary exercise which applies the theory of elasticity of demand and supply, and we can readily reproduce the simple diagram to show the answer (see Fig. 1). Our treatment of this question can be very simple indeed. We do not need to show any figures involved if we so choose. By using the graph we can say that the new and higher price of wine will not exceed the previous equilibrium by the full amount of the tax. *lm* is the amount of the tax paid by the consumer and *mn* the share paid by the seller. In doing this exercise we have indulged in a few steps of logic. Propositions are made and conclusions are drawn: (a) the rise in tax causes an upward shift of the supply curve because at all

95

existing prices producers are obliged to charge more in order to receive the same amount for selling a certain quantity before the tax was imposed; (b) a new (higher) equilibrium price will be reached where the new (higher) supply curve intersects the demand curve. We then (c) calculate how much the new price is higher than the original equilibrium. We see that (d) if it is not higher by the total amount of the tax then the full burden is not carried by the seller and thus the amount that the new price exceeds the old one is the extra cost to the consumer. Thus if the original equilibrium were 70p. and the sales tax of 5p. caused a final equilibrium price of 73p. then 3p. of the tax is carried by the consumer and 2p. by the seller. The point we would hope to put over to our pupils is that the incidence of the tax, i.e. the distribution of the tax burden between customer and seller, depends upon the elasticities of demand and supply for the product. More precisely it depends upon the ratio of the elasticity of demand to the elasticity of supply and the more the elasticity of supply exceeds that of demand the more of the tax burden can the seller pass on to the consumer. Having got this far our next step would probably be to calculate the elasticity of demand between the prices 70p. and 73p., and most of us would use, for this purpose, the formula:

$$\text{elasticity of demand} = \frac{\% \text{ change in quantity}}{\% \text{ change in price}}$$

if we assume the original equilibrium quantity sold to be 3,400 and the new quantity sold after tax imposition to be 2,700, we would work out the elasticity of demand as follows:

$$\frac{\% \text{ change in quantity}}{\% \text{ change in price}} = \frac{\dfrac{700}{3400} \times \dfrac{100}{1}}{\dfrac{3}{70} \times \dfrac{100}{1}} = \frac{700 \times 7}{34 \times 30} = \frac{490}{102} = 4 \cdot 8$$

and we would show to our pupils that, since the proportionate change in quantity exceeds the proportionate change in price, then demand for this commodity is elastic between the two prices.

We can say the same thing another way by using equations. If we define x as the original quantity, then the new quantity demanded can be defined as $x + \Delta x$, where Δ means 'a small increase in'. Similarly, with p as the original price, then $p + \Delta p$ is the change in

96

price. The proportionate change in price is written as $\Delta p/p$, whilst the proportionate change in quantity as $\Delta x/x$. Thus the elasticity of demand is the ratio of the proportionate change in quantity to the proportionate change in price, that is:

$$\frac{\Delta x}{x} \div \frac{\Delta p}{p}$$

using the symbol ε_D to mean elasticity of demand and dividing the two fractions we have:

(1) $$\varepsilon_D = \frac{p\Delta x}{x\Delta p}$$

Substituting figures we find that our answer is the same as that gained from our well-known method. The answer, 5, shows that the proportionate change in quantity is greater than the proportionate change in price and thus demand is elastic. Thus:

$$\varepsilon_D = \frac{70 \times 700}{3400 \times 3} = \frac{490}{102} = 4 \cdot 8$$

We would then, no doubt, state or revise the propositions that different degrees of elasticity exist with two main subdivisions, elastic and inelastic, expressed numerically as greater than one (elastic) or less than one (inelastic). These two propositions can be expressed in equations:

(2) $$\frac{\Delta x}{x} > \frac{\Delta p}{p} \text{ then } \varepsilon_D > 1 \quad \text{i.e. is elastic}$$

(3) $$\frac{\Delta x}{x} < \frac{\Delta p}{p} \text{ then } \varepsilon_D < 1 \quad \text{i.e. is inelastic}$$

We would probably all agree that equation (2) is a far simpler way of stating the proportion than is the verbal 'Where the proportionate change in the quantity bought exceeds the proportionate change in the price, then elasticity of demand is greater than one, that is, it is elastic.'

Similarly the elasticity of supply would be calculated in the same way. Thus:

(4) $$\varepsilon_s = \frac{p\Delta x}{x\Delta p}$$

In this case p does not take into account the 5p. tax and therefore p is -2.

$$\varepsilon_s = \frac{70 \times 700}{3400 \times 2} = \frac{490}{68} = 7.2$$

The fact that the elasticity of supply (7·2) exceeds the elasticity of demand (4·8) shows that the greater burden of the tax can be passed on to the consumer. However the closeness of the two elasticities shows that the seller has very little lee-way and will have to shoulder a considerable part of the burden himself.

In this example we started from a very simple situation, the imposition of a tax. We asked our pupils to calculate the incidence of the tax and to calculate how effective it would be as a means of raising revenue. What we found was that the tax incidence fell more upon the consumer (by just over a half) than on the seller and that the imposition of the tax caused demand to fall off by a greater proportion than the price change. Demand was elastic. The tax on wine has caused wine consumption to fall (from 3,400 to 2,700 units per week) but has it caused the total expenditure on wine to fall? Also (a question we raised earlier), how effective has it been in taking purchasing power out of the public's pockets? Again to answer these questions we use arithmetic and some simple algebra. We have at our disposal concepts, the one which is most useful at this stage being that of total revenue (TR), which is calculated by multiplying the quantity sold (Q) by the price (P). Thus:

$$TR = P \times Q$$

At the original equilibrium price TR was 238,000 pence per week ($70 \times 3,400$). At the higher price caused as a result of the tax, total expenditure, or total revenue as far as the industry is concerned, is 197,000 pence per week (73p. $\times 2,700$). We must also remember that 13,500 pence per week must be deducted from this latter total since this is the amount of tax collected by the government. What now remains to the wine trade is $197,000 - 13,500 = 183,500$ pence per week. We find that as a result of this tax the wine trade is considerably worse off than before.

Has this tax been a good means of raising revenue? Yes, to the extent that there are now 13,500 pence per week where the government had none before (yielding £7,020 extra per annum). But is this good? The answer must be No! As a result of the tax demand fell considerably, i.e. people preferred not to purchase wine at the higher price, they held on to their purchasing power. The government was not able to mop up much excess. The turnover of the wine trade, after tax, was considerably lower than before (183,500 pence compared to 197,000 pence) which means less corporation tax, since the incidence of tax fell heavily upon the seller as well as the consumer. The demand was elastic (4·8) as was the supply (7·2), and for purposes of raising revenue the government would have been wise to consider taxing a commodity the demand for which was inelastic where:

$$\frac{\Delta x}{x} \div \frac{\Delta p}{p} < 1$$

Can your pupils tell you why? And can they suggest any commodities? All the tax has done is to reduce wine consumption, probably to the benefit of beer (again can your pupil say why?).

To do this exercise in Applied Economics which examines tax incidence, tax effects *vis-à-vis* deflation and any social effects, we have used a few tools – simple arithmetic and a number of formulae to help us to remember what aspect of theory to apply to the situation. None of this is complex. We feel that this can be a useful tool to your pupils but especially as a teaching aid to yourself.

Let us take another presentation of another well-known concept, this time in the field of macro-economics – the identity of national expenditure, national income and national output and the proposition that equilibrium level of income is where they equal each other.

We will establish fairly quickly to our pupils that this equality is not simultaneous – income, expenditure and output do not equal each other at the same time – they are equal *ex post*, not necessarily are they equal *ex ante* (the same being true of saving and investment). We mean by this that expenditure at one period of time will determine income in the next, and that income in turn will determine the level of expenditure. Instead of $E = Y$ (E expenditure and Y income) we have, as Lipsey puts it, $Et = Yt+1$, i.e. the level of expenditure at one period of time will determine the level of income in the next. If expenditure falls income will be lower – a fundamental point of Keynesian Economics which is saying that the level of income depends upon expenditure, i.e. effective demand. In its turn effective demand is made up of consumption, investment, government expenditure and exports, or $(Y = C+I+G+X)$. We will explain this relationship of effective demand and its components to our pupils, and we will explain to them what each of the components depends upon.

(a) $C = f(Y)$ – consumption is a function of (i.e. depends upon) income.

(b) $I = f(\text{MEC}, r, \Delta C)$ – investment depends upon the marginal efficiency of capital, the rate of interest and the rate of change in consumption (accelerator principle).

(c) G is largely autonomous, decisions to spend being in the hands of politicians.

(d) $X = f(Y°)$ – expenditure on exports depends upon overseas incomes.

From these shorthand expressions of our concepts we progress to study each in detail. What does consumption depend upon? Answer: the level of income. We construct a consumption function to show our pupils what this means. Here we are using a simple two-

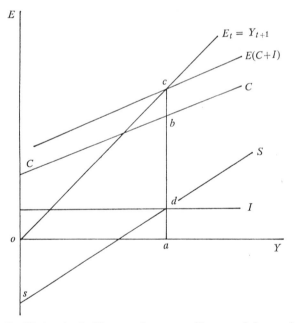

Fig. 2. Equilibrium level of income where expenditure equals income ($oa = ac$).

dimensional illustration (see Fig. 2). We show the amount of consumption at each level of income and from this we can deduce another important concept – that as income rises consumption does not increase proportionately. More is saved, i.e. the vertical difference between CC and the 45° line $E = Y$ increases. If the level of income were oa, then ab would be spent on consumption leaving bc a surplus, i.e. saved (saving defined as what is left of income after consumption has taken place). If $Y = E$, as we have proposed (more exactly $Et = Yt + 1$) then the savings must be used for some purpose if equilibrium is to be maintained. The answer, we know, is investment which we can show initially as a horizontal line (implying it does not vary with income – this is for simplicity in the initial stages). Since $S = I$ then the gap cb equals da (the level of investment) and our simple model is in equilibrium with $E = Y$. But suppose investment were not equal to saving. Here we would have total expenditure ($C + I$ for simplification's sake) less than the total income, a situation which is disequilibrium and, since $Et = Yt + 1$, we can show that income will fall until it equals expenditure at a lower level. We would hope to show to our pupils that the reduced income will cause lower savings.

We have now used an important concept, the multiplier, without having named it. This is based on a straightforward concept that a person spends part of extra income that he receives but does not spend all of it. The greater the proportion of extra income he spends, the more will another receive, and if the recipient spends the same proportion then the total level of income will go on increasing, but not by the same amount (in pounds), but by the same proportion until (theoretically) the last (say) 80% of a penny is spent. We will show that a given increase in income, say as a result of an investment project or a tax cut, will increase final income by a multiple. The amount by which the final income is raised will depend upon what proportion of additional income is spent on consumption, i.e. it will depend upon the marginal propensity to consume (MPC) from which we calculate the multiplier.

We have a number of ways at our disposal to illustrate the point to our pupils. Firstly an arithmetical one. Assume an MPC of four-fifths and an initial injection of an extra £100,000,000 into the economy, say on motorway construction. We can build up a table to show the multiplier effect in the following way:

	(a) Income	(b) Expenditure ($\frac{4}{5}$)	(c) Saving ($\frac{1}{5}$)
(1)	100,000,000 ———⟶	80,000,000 ————	⟶ 20,000,000
(2)	80,000,000 ⟵— ——⟶	64,000,000 ————	⟶ 16,000,000
(3)	64,000,000 ⟵— ——⟶	43,200,000 ————	⟶ 10,800,000
(4)	43,000,000 ⟵— ——⟶	34,560,000 ————	⟶ 8,640,000
	Continued with $\frac{4}{5}$ consumed and $\frac{1}{5}$ saved.		
Total	500,000,000	400,000,000	100,000,000

and so the progression goes until the last four-fifths of the last pound is spent and one-fifth saved. We find that in adding up total income generated in column (a) we have a multiple of five times the original investment injection, whilst in adding up column (c) we have a sum equal to the original investment. Our illustration has shown two things, firstly that the rise in income is greater than the original rise in investment, and secondly that saving has increased to equal the original investment. Two important points are thereby illustrated, firstly the multiplier effect and secondly the equality of saving and investment as a result of an *ex post* increase in income. Can we expect our pupils to deduce the size of the multiplier from this example? Perhaps. They will need some prompting – it bears a relation to the proportion saved, in that the increase in income is five times higher than the original injection, whilst the proportion saved out of every additional increase in income is one-fifth. Is it enough to say then 'therefore the multiplier is five, i.e. it is the reciprocal of the marginal propensity to save'? Could we so easily calculate the multiplier if the marginal propensity to save were two-sevenths?

We can make our point about the multiplier effect perfectly clearly to our pupils by the above example. It has shown them the points we intended. We have shown the derivation of the multiplier, but it has taken a long-winded example. Again we have an alternative, with a simple formula as an *aide memoire*. Firstly let us give the multiplier a symbol, k. Then we define it as the ratio between the increase in income and the increase in investment:

(1) $$k = \frac{\Delta Y}{\Delta I}$$

102

We know that, in order to calculate the multiplier, we must know the marginal propensity to consume or the marginal propensity to save. We can define the former as:

(2) $\qquad \dfrac{\Delta C}{\Delta Y}$ i.e. the increase in consumption as result of an increase in income

We define the marginal propensity to save, for which we use the symbol s, as:

(3) $$s = 1 - \frac{\Delta C}{\Delta Y}$$

Since the increase in income is made up of the increase in consumption plus the increase in investment (the latter can be written as $\Delta I = 1 - C$), we can rewrite equation (3) as:

(4) $$\frac{1}{s} = \frac{\Delta Y}{\Delta I}$$

The right-hand side of this equation has already been defined as the multiplier in equation (1), thus we can say:

(5) $$k = \frac{1}{s}$$

which is the same as the more-often used formula:

(6) $$k = \frac{1}{\text{MPS}} = \frac{1}{1 - \text{MPC}}$$

In this example it can be firmly argued that the derivation of the multiplier is a waste of time. We can teach our Economics perfectly well without this presentation, but if the derivation helps to make the point more clearly, then it is useful. We must bear in mind that the algebraic equations are a shorthand form of an hypothesis. They do not necessarily prove the point, although the use of mathematical proofs is common and is becoming increasingly so.

A useful classroom exercise is to try to find a local example of this multiplier effect – say the opening of a new factory with 100 jobs paying £20 per week. How much would this raise the level of income in the town or community as a whole? Your example would have to be a highly simplified one, in which you assume at first a highly closed economy with no leakages such as government taxation or spending outside the community, but nonetheless it can serve to illustrate the point. The factory, in this example, would inject initially a sum of £2,000 per week into the community. Assuming a constant marginal propensity to consume of four-fifths, the marginal propensity to save is thus one-fifth and the multiplier is accordingly 5, that is:

$$k = \frac{1}{s} = 1/\tfrac{1}{5} = 5$$

Total community income will rise by £10,000 per week or by £500,000 per annum. If time allows try to calculate a realistic multiplier by taking account of the normal leakages from the income flow, including government and local taxation, expenditure on foreign goods as well as expenditure outside the locality. An even more dramatic example of the multiplier and one which would help to explain why depressed areas tend to stay depressed would be to try to calculate the multiplier effect of, for example, pit closures in an area. If we took as an example a colliery employing 500 workers and paying out average wages of £20 per head per week, and assumed the marginal propensities to consume and to save as being the same as in the previous example, then we would find that the community was now £50,000 per week worse off as a result of this initial loss of income (again this is a highly simplified example). Despite the simplicity of these examples they can be used to illustrate basic principles, such as why the need for new industries in coal-mining regions is pressing or why boom areas such as the midlands or the south-east go on booming and attracting new industry.

Many teachers will have little or no formal education in Mathematics above ordinary level but, since they are conversant with the theories of Economics, they should understand the mathematical presentations which some books adopt. We have argued in another section that we consider Mathematics an important subject to be studied at Advanced level with Economics and we have advocated studying it at additional 'O' level to supplement the main course, but even pupils who are not following these disciplines should not be debarred from being taught the mathematical approach. The use of Mathematics is rapidly establishing itself in all the Social Sciences and this approach must eventually filter down to the schools. For the teacher we realise that learning the use of mathematical tools may present some difficulties but these can be solved fairly easily. Firstly, the level of work is not high. You are already economists and are familiar with the concepts being discussed. If you are fortunate enough to be one of a number of economists in a department organise yourselves into a study group and work through an elementary mathematical economics textbook – say Archibald and Lipsey, or Dowsett. You can always take difficult problems along to a member of the Mathematics staff. You can work with a book on your own, or with your pupils, especially if some are studying 'A' level Mathematics. You can also go on vacation courses run by extra-mural departments of the universities where the use of Mathematics in Economics is one of the topics being studied, for example the regular summer conference held at Bath University of Technology.

We would recommend some of the following texts as useful for your reading and teaching – Archibald and Lipsey, *Introduction to Mathematical Economics*, Weidenfeld and Nicholson, 1967; Parry-Lewis, *An Introduction to Mathematics for Students of Economics*, Papermac, 1967; and Dowsett, *Elementary Mathematics in Economics*, Pitman.

We would add in conclusion that we are aware that many Economics teachers, brought up on a non-mathematical approach to Economics, feel that although the mathematical approach is desirable it is beyond them. Our experience suggests that in many cases this need not be so and that the initial effort to master these techniques is well worth while.

7

ECONOMICS IN THE GENERAL STUDIES COURSE

The role of the economics course

Part of the post-war revolution in education has been concerned with the introduction of General or Liberal Studies into the sixth-form curriculum. The development of general courses has been somewhat haphazard and consequently the structure of the courses varies tremendously from school to school. In some schools a course has evolved from the general interests, outside their own academic disciplines, of the teachers within the schools. In others it has been rigorously designed as a formal element in the sixth-form curriculum. No matter what the structure of the General Studies course it is almost axiomatic that an important role has been allotted to the teaching of Social Science and thus a course in basic Economics is frequently included.

The structure of the Economics for General Studies course itself varies widely, depending largely upon the interests of the teacher and upon the time given to Economics in the General Studies time-table. We may summarise the kinds of situation in which the student of other disciplines may find himself face to face with information of an economic nature in the interest of furthering his general education. Within the General Studies framework Economics appears in several different guises:

(a) As the formal but non-specialised course outlining the structure of the British economy, the institutions through which it operates and its problems.

(b) As a background study to students' special subjects, which examines specific topics in some depth, e.g. 'The location and structure of British industries', for Geography students or 'The economics of industry', for students of Physics and Chemistry.

(c) As part of an Environmental Studies course where pupils are encouraged to find out about their own immediate environment from such different aspects as geographical evolution, historical development and social and economic activities.

(d) As part of a team teaching project as, for instance, in a course on the cinema, the Economics teacher may be asked to lecture on 'The economics of film-making', or 'The effects of a declining cinema-going population'.

(e) As a current affairs lesson.

Wherever the Economics teacher is underemployed he is likely to find all kinds of topics on his General Studies timetable, sometimes inherited from a teacher who left the school the previous term. These topics will fall between the two traditional spheres of 'arts' and 'sciences' and will include everything from 'The novels of Kafka', to 'Water pollution in the Deccan' or 'The social psychology of the Incas'.

Designing the scheme of work

Within the limits of any General Studies course each Economics teacher will be responsible for producing his own scheme of work. The scheme he produces will be the result of many factors – his own particular interests, whether he is working towards an examination in General Studies, the size of his class, the number of lessons he has at his disposal each week and so on. Above all the scheme must be relevant to the needs and interests of the particular group of pupils. For the teacher's guidance we present three different schemes of work which have been used successfully.

A. THE BRITISH ECONOMY

A survey of the structure of the economy, its institutions and its problems. Here we assume that the teacher is faced with organising a course of one half year's duration with one forty-minute lesson per week (i.e. approximately twenty lessons) to be given to a group of fifteen pupils studying between them a wide variety of subjects to 'A' level, but excluding Economics.

Lessons 1 and 2. The economic problem
The concepts of scarcity and choice; how different societies attempt to solve them; capitalism, totalitarianism, social democracy.

107

Discussion. (In each case the questions listed may be used for written work or for class discussion.) Is it possible for individual nations to solve the basic economic problem or must the solution be an international achievement?

Lessons 3, 4, 5 and 6. *The concept of national income*

Lesson 3. Everyone has a dual economic role – as an earner and as a spender of income. The simple domestic economy; households and firms; the flow of incomes, goods and services; a simple view of the process of income formation.

Lessons 4 and 5. The national income of a 'welfare' economy; households, firms, government and the rest of the world; how government income and expenditure and how trading relations with the rest of the world modify the model of the 'simple domestic economy'. The growing importance of U.K. government expenditure since 1906. The main items of national income and expenditure.

Lesson 6. Significant statistical data to illustrate the size of the U.K. national income; the growth of national income in the twentieth century; comparisons with the national incomes of India and the U.S.A.; relative sizes of the populations of U.K., India and U.S.A.; differences in the sizes of incomes per head of the populations. The relative sizes of U.K. public and private sector expenditure; consumption and investment expenditure; income from abroad and expenditure abroad.

Discussion. (i) What different ways are there in which incomes are obtained? Does the way in which an individual obtains his income tell us anything about the way in which he is likely to spend it?

(ii) Do government policies generally help or hinder the flow of national income?

(iii) Should we all spend our holidays in Britain?

(iv) From the data supplied draw graphs to illustrate the growth of private, public and national expenditure in the U.K. from 1900.

(v) How can the national income of the U.K. be increased?

Lesson 7. *Demand and consumption*

The transactions, precautionary and speculative motives for holding money; different kinds of consumption expenditure; consumption and the pattern of consumption a function of income; social patterns of consumption and saving.

Discussion. Build up a weekly budget for two families, consisting in each case of a man, wife, two children, dog, buying their houses on mortgage and cars on hire purchase, with a weekly income in one case of £22 and in the other of £220.

Lessons 8 and 9. *Saving and investment*

How saving arises and how it becomes investment; the chief sources of investment in the U.K.: undistributed profits, government expenditure, insurance companies, building societies, the banks, the stock market; the rate of interest.

Discussion. As a bank manager, give reasoned advice to the people listed below on how to obtain the largest and safest returns on their savings:

(a) A 20-year-old maintenance engineer, who has recently completed his apprenticeship. He is engaged to be married and is earning £900 per annum.

(b) A 62-year-old widow, whose husband has left her a house, £4,000 in cash and an annuity of £250 per annum.

(c) A 40-year-old solicitor, with a wife and two children, one aged twelve, the other seventeen. He has an income of £4000 per annum.

108

ECONOMICS IN THE GENERAL STUDIES COURSE

Lessons 10 and 11. Supply and production

Large and small firms; their organisation; specific examples of each type. The factors of production; the costs of production; fixed and variable costs; their relative importance in different types of industry. The market; supply and demand schedules.

Discussion. From data given draw up supply and demand schedules for different goods and show the market prices and quantities sold.

Lesson 12. Employment

The level of employment, investment and the multiplier effect. The standard of living; why unemployment occurs.

Discussion. How can we explain the differences in standards of living between developed and underdeveloped nations? What form should aid to the underdeveloped nations take?

Lesson 13, 14 and 15. The institutions of the economy

Lesson 13. The money market; the Bank of England, the commercial banks, hire purchase, the quantity of money and credit, price levels.

Lesson 14. The capital market; Stock Exchange, banks, building societies, insurance companies, investment trusts.

Lesson 15. The foreign exchange market; the International Monetary Fund, exchange equalisation account, balance of trade and payments, devaluation.

Discussion. (i) Why does a rise in the 'bank rate' of the U.S.A. sometimes cause an increase in the U.K. mortgage rates of interest?

(ii) Why has Britain devalued twice since 1945?

(iii) Argue the case for and against the introduction of decimal coinage.

Lessons 16 and 17. The role of the government in controlling the level of economic activity

The relationships between government departments concerned with economic affairs; the Treasury; taxation and the budget; nationalised industries.

Discussion. (i) Does increasing government control hinder the economic freedom of the individual?

(ii) Are present levels of taxation a disincentive?

(iii) Should nationalised industries pay their way?

Lessons 18 and 19

Analysis and discussion of current economic problems; e.g. a recent balance of payments crisis, development areas, industrial relations, restrictive practices.

Lesson 20. Testing

A test using objective-type techniques involving working out simple numerical problems, completing diagrams and giving 'one word' answers. About 50 questions in all.

Reading

Gertrude Williams, *The Economics of Everyday Life*, Penguin

G. W. R. Geary, *The Background of Business*, Oxford

P. Donaldson, *Guide to the British Economy*, Penguin

G. Smith, *Britain's Economy*, Mills and Boon

Handbook of Britain, current ed., H.M.S.O.

Films to use

	Title	Production company	Distributor
Lesson 10	*Enterprise*	I.C.I.	I.C.I. Film Library
	Portrait of a Man	Unilever	Unilever Film Library
Lesson 11	*Balance, 1950*	I.C.I.	I.C.I. Film Library
	Point of Sale		
Lesson 13	*The Bank of England*	Bank of England	Rank Film Library
	The Rise of Parnassus	Barclay's Bank	
	Needy		
Lesson 14	*The Launching*	Stock Exchange	Rank Film Library
Lesson 15	*The Pilgrim*	Barclay's Bank	Sound Services Ltd.
Lesson 16	*The Signs and*		
	Portents	I.C.I.	I.C.I. Film Library

All available on 16 mm sound, free loan.

B. THE ECONOMICS OF INDUSTRY

This scheme of work has been used for a course on 'The economics of industry' for a group of science pupils studying mainly Physics, Chemistry and Mathematics to 'A' level. Eventually most of these pupils will be employed by large industrial firms in research, scientific management or production engineering. The teacher is faced with organising a one-term course (ten double lessons each of seventy minutes duration) for a group of twenty pupils.

Lesson 1

The development of technology in Britain since the Industrial Revolution; the present location of the major industries in Britain. The factors of production; changes in their relative importance as the scale of industry has increased; the division of labour, specialisation of function, automation, the computer revolution.

Lesson 2

The finance of production; the costs of industry, the relation between fixed and variable costs; the relation between costs and price. Large and small firms. Competitive markets.

Lesson 3

The market. Perfect competition – an economic model. The real world situation – monopolistic competition.

Lessons 4 and 5

Oligopoly, specific examples of this type of market structure. Oligopoly becoming the predominant form of market. The full cost principle; price discrimination; non-price competition with particular reference to advertising. Price rigidity and resale price maintenance.

ECONOMICS IN THE GENERAL STUDIES COURSE

Lesson 6

Industry, and government; market competition and the law; investment problems; labour relations.

Lessons 7, 8, 9 and 10. A case study (I.C.I.)

Origins and growth of the firm; its structure and organisation; its wide variety of products, production techniques, marketing and distribution at home and abroad. Problems of production, e.g. abolition of resale price maintenance, mobility of labour and manpower policy.

Reading

Challoner and Musson, *Industry and Technology*, Studio Vista.
E. A. G. Robinson, *The Structure of Competitive Industry*, C.U.P.
Handbook of Britain, H.M.S.O.

Films to use

Balance, 1950	
Enterprise	I.C.I. Film Library
Estimating Profits by Computer	
Point of Sale	
The Power We Need	National Coal Board Film Library
Outline of Detergency	Unilever Film Library
River of Steel	British Iron and Steel Federation

All available on 16 mm sound, free loan.

C. A GENERAL ECONOMICS COURSE

Here the assumption is that the class will have twenty forty-minute periods in one term and that there will be no examination. The students will be taking other subjects at 'A' level or are spending a year in the sixth form without the G.C.E. in mind. The aim is to interest them in Economics by bringing out the fact that when they leave school they will have to earn a living in a given state of the economy and therefore a knowledge of Economics is important to them no matter what occupation they follow. A textbook is not necessary, but it is recommended that they be advised and encouraged to read any one of several introductions to Economics. A reasonably well stocked library of journals and newspaper cuttings should be available.

Lessons 1 and 2 should deal with the need to earn a living, using factors that are relatively scarce and have alternative uses, hence opportunity costs, particularly the hard fact that if you have this, you must give up that. Discuss the nature of work, in the sense that it involves self-discipline, going to the office or the factory at hours when the worker would rather be enjoying his leisure.

Lessons 3 and 4 should be a description of the United Kingdom economy today, an open, mixed economy, with a very high degree of industrialisation as

111

well as specialisation, in which the use of capital is intensive, productivity per man is high but not high enough, wages are high, yet there is a continuous demand for higher wages.

Lessons 5 and 6 could raise the question of self-interest and the profit motive; is this the most efficient way of making the most of resources; does it create a materialistic outlook on life that creates an unhealthy rivalry resulting in a socially unjust distribution of wealth which is largely in the hands of a few people?

Lessons 7 and 8 could examine the rise of the Welfare State, with its governmental planning institutions, anti-monopoly measures, progressive taxation, social services producing desired utility, the creation of nationalised industries that aim to render services rather than make profits.

Lessons 9 and 10 should introduce the use of money, its functions, the growth of banking, the distinction between real wealth and income and money wealth and income; the essence of this part of the course should be to dispel the monetary illusions.

Lessons 11 and 12 must bring out the conflicts within the economy, the ambivalent relationships between employers and trade unions, the effect of taxes upon a man's freedom to spend his money as he likes, the tendency to inflation if there is full employment, hence the need for a wage freeze and a Prices and Incomes Board, and so on.

Lessons 13 and 14 should explain why the United Kingdom needs to export and to import, the problem of the balance of payments, the need for an international central bank with an international currency, the use of gold for this purpose, and so on.

Lessons 15 and 16 can expound the national income, the reasons why this calculation is made, the propensity to consume and to save, the importance of using savings to pay for investment in real capital, the cost of living and the standard of living, index numbers.

Lessons 17 and 18 might discuss the relationship between leisure and work, the importance of using leisure constructively and of not regarding it merely as an opportunity to be idle, the kind of job that the students get when he leaves school, what is a good job, etc.

Lessons 19 and 20 will be a review of the course, an opportunity to clear up misunderstandings, but also a chance to explain how to open a bank account and take out an insurance policy, the advantages and disadvantages of hire purchase, how to buy a house with the aid of a mortgage, the functions of a trade union, and so on.

Finally you should keep the course flexible, twist it and turn it to your own experience as you go on. You will find that some topics rouse such lively discussion that you give extra time to them.

Problems and teaching method

These suggested schemes of work pose certain problems in their operation and presuppose the use of certain teaching techniques. In this final section we hope to expose and clarify some of these problems and methods.

The two chief enemies of the teacher of General Studies are time and apathy. One or two lessons per week are never enough for him to feel that he can communicate some difficult ideas to a class of arts specialists, especially when he has been enjoying up to eight lessons a week with his specialist Economics class. Additionally, the teacher's first reaction to his realisation that the class has no real interest in his subject and would much rather be doing private study, is to feel rather hurt. On reflection, he will have to admit that such a situation presents a formidable challenge to his teaching ability, and, if he is able, in a short course, to cover a great deal of ground, to make the class feel that they have achieved something important and to bring them to the point where they are anxious to discuss economic affairs, he has gained a notable personal triumph.

To be successful the teacher must be a master of diplomacy: he must know almost instinctively when to use 'chalk and talk' and when to show the class a film, when to refrain from comment during class discussions, when to set written exercises and how many of them to impose. He must be willing to spend, initially, an hour's preparation for a forty-minute lesson. He must know when too deep an analysis of a problem will prove a hindrance to a pupil's understanding. Ideally he should have technical equipment and the ability to use it effectively. He could make good use of a 16-mm sound film projector, a room that can be blacked out, an overhead projector, a typewriter and access to duplicating and photocopying machines.

Thus the basic answer to the problems associated with the lack of teaching time and the apathy of pupils lies in the meticulous preparation of lessons. Lecture to a General Studies class as little as possible and only when there is no other effective method of teaching. Some lecturing is of course unavoidable, but the aim should be to involve the class in some form of active participation as often as can be managed. For instance, duplicate a diagram of the operation of a 'welfare' economy or the relations between the government departments concerned with economic policy and base your lesson entirely on the diagram, and inviting observations and comments from the class. Prepare and duplicate statistical tables. Ask the class to prepare graphs to illustrate the statistical data and to comment on the graphs. Do not be afraid to show films in class. Some that may be found suitable are listed at the end of each scheme of work above. Some films for example, *The Bank of England* can be shown without comment unless the class wish to discuss it afterwards. *Balance, 1950* is an animated film, made by I.C.I., to explain the company's balance sheet to their employees and is able to do in nine minutes what it could well take a lecturer several lessons to explain. *Signs and Portents* is another I.C.I. film showing aspects of the relationship between government and industry. All these and others such as *The Rise of Parnassus Needy*, a cartoon about borrowing money from a bank, have an important impact in General Studies teaching. In a General Studies course, drawing diagrams on a blackboard can be a time-wasting form of communication. Diagrams are of course valuable aids to teaching in Economics and, if a diagram is to form a basis of the lesson, duplicate enough copies for the class. If it is a diagram used to illustrate and explain one particular point then draw it beforehand either on the blackboard or to show on an overhead projector.

Recommend the class to read specified sections or chapters in books rather than the whole book; and make sure that the books you recommend are readily available, either in the school or public library. Introduce them to specific articles in 'quality' newspapers, for example William Davis who writes occasionally in *The Guardian* has an amazing facility for clear and simple presentation of economic problems and policies without understating the situation. Try to ensure that any initial efforts that the class make for themselves are immediately successful so that they gain a sense of achievement and progress. If they are encouraged and if they make progress their initial apathy will rapidly disappear. It is worthwhile buying several copies of each of *The Economics of Everyday Life*, *Guide to the British Economy* and the *Economist* pamphlets on 'Devaluation' for the use of the General Studies group alone. Do not, on the other hand, recommend the class to read the more difficult or 'drier' Economics textbooks that they will not be able to understand at the first reading.

Encourage discussion, remembering that, outside their own special studies, pupils may well be hesitant to state their opinions. It helps in this respect if groups of pupils are kept down to a reasonable size. Ten is an ideal number, fifteen is probably the number you can expect to have, and anything above twenty is far too large.

The opinions they do advance will be those they have gained from their parents, from the popular press and from party political broadcasts. Their opinions will be based on political rather than on economic criteria. The teacher ought not to refute these opinions outright nor pour scorn on what he may regard as ideas which do not make economic sense if he wishes to gain the confidence, enthusiasm and co-operation of his pupils.

There should be some written work which will help the pupil to judge his grasp of the subject and, to this end, it should be set on a practical basis involving, for example, the collection and summary of data, drawing graphs, solving specific problems both numerical in character and those posed in a given situation. However, an overload of written work to be completed out of class, perhaps at the expense of 'A' level work, can only lead to resentment closely followed by a return to apathy. It is very often useful to the pupils if you prepare summary sheets of the lessons you give. These should be distributed at the end of the lesson; they will enable the class to maintain its interest despite the tremendous pace of the course. It will give them something to go through in the minutes before the lesson begins to remind them of the work done in the previous lesson and it will help the occasional absentee to keep up with the course.

It is rarely necessary or even desirable to teach the tools of economic analysis in detail to a General Studies class. It is enough to give them a general view of consumer behaviour in terms of the social patterns of consumption without trying to teach a full-scale indifference curve analysis. Make the course an outline of what you consider are the essential facts. A series of maps to show the location of the major industries of the U.K. is preferable to a detailed analysis involving an understanding of the theory of the location of industry.

Teaching Economics to General Studies pupils can be a rewarding experience as well as a severe test of teaching ability. If, like us, you believe that everyone should have a basic knowledge of economic affairs you may come to regard the General Studies lessons as an opportunity to join a crusade rather than an attempt by your headmaster to prevent you enjoying too many free periods – but the crusading spirit makes great demands upon a teacher's time, enthusiasm and ingenuity. If we have anticipated in this chapter some of the difficulties and questions which you will encounter in organising a scheme of work for Economics in the General Studies course we have done something to engender a spirit that will bring an increasing number of pupils to a better understanding of economic affairs.

8

BRITISH CONSTITUTION

Although this book is primarily concerned with comments and suggestions about the teaching of Economics, it was thought that there was a case for including a chapter on a subject which can often be related to Economics – British Constitution. The subject is sometimes called Government or Public Administration or Political Affairs. It is likely that most teachers of Economics will have had some education in Political Science as part of their degree course and we feel that if you are not already required to teach British Constitution you may want to introduce the subject into your school's curriculum. We know of one master who, in order to get the subject established, agreed to teach it for twenty minutes each week to a selected group of sixth formers during morning assembly on Fridays. His experiment succeeded and the subject became accepted into the curriculum. We are not advising that teachers break the rules of the 1944 Education Act as he did, though we approve of the enthusiasm.

The role of the subject in the curriculum

The decade from 1956 to 1966 saw an enormous expansion in the number of candidates studying both subjects at Advanced and Ordinary levels, and during this period the number of 'A' level passes attained in Economics and British Constitution increased almost sixfold from 2,944 to 17,501. The importance attached to the two subjects can be seen if compared to the total of passes in Geography in 1966, which at 17,645 was only slightly larger. *Statistics of Education*, 1966, vol. 2, H.M.S.O., from which the above figures are taken, shows that the increase in the number of candidates passing Economics and British Constitution is greater than that of any subject. The number of candidates taking History increased by 130·9% and Geography by 182·0%. The table below shows the number of entries for 'A' level in 1966. It shows that, as yet, British

Constitution is in its infancy but is, nonetheless, a robust babe and has every possibility of growing to considerable stature.

Subject	Entries	% passed	% of A's	S. paper (total)
Economics	17,341	60·0	6·5	1,444
British Constitution	9,098	56·0	4·3	59
History	31,043	71·6	9·0	4,295
Geography	25,389	69·5	8·7	2,541
Maths. (Pure)	15,311	65·3	9·5	1,434
Maths. (Pure and Applied)	26,771	66·2	9·1	2,178

There does seem to be a very good case why boys studying Economics should find British Constitution a very useful complement. Indeed, the mutual relationship of the subjects is recognised by certain of the examination boards by making Economics and Government, or Politics into a combined paper. Because of this close relationship we would raise the question as to whether or not the approach to teaching British Constitution should be any different from teaching Economics. The use of press cuttings, the importance of outside visits and the writing of informed essays are common to both subjects in which an awareness of current events is vital. We feel, however, that there are some fundamental differences, the main one being that wider reading in British Constitution is undertaken from the start. Whilst some teachers of Economics may want their pupils to use only one textbook in the first year in order to avoid confusion of concepts which may be presented differently by various authors; others tend to introduce reading more cautiously, indicating at first specific pages to be read from a variety of books, later recommending specific chapters and eventually simply recommending books that the pupils ought to read or merely look at. Later in the second year even wider reading is urged on the pupils who by this time are familiar with the terminology and the essential theories of the subject. The same teachers, however, when teaching British Constitution urge their pupils to read widely and generally from the start, getting away from basic texts and reading informed commentaries, political biographies and autobiographies and political novels. We say more on the subject of books later in this chapter.

With two-fifths of the gross national product being spent by the

117

state, it is impossible today to understand the economic system without knowing a good deal about the system of government which is responsible for such a large part of it. Many topics, such as public finance, the control of monopolies and the structure of public corporations are common to both fields of study. The close link was perhaps made clearer when Economics was known generally as Political Economy, and this link between Economics and Political Studies is maintained at university level. Nor is the state concerned in the economy merely as a spender and as a participant in the productive process. It is generally recognised that, after the office of Prime Minister, that of Chancellor of the Exchequer is next in importance, whilst the Treasury remains the most important of all government departments and the Prime Minister still holds the title of its First Lord. The Board of Trade, a department concerned with the regulation of commerce and industry, is old-established and many illustrious politicians have held the Presidency. In recent years we have seen the creation of new departments and ministries, such as the Department of Economic Affairs and the Ministry of Technology, as well as the creation of official bodies such as the Prices and Incomes Board and the National Economic Development Council. In this post-Keynesian society the government has become the overall planner, accepting responsibility for directing and planning the economy, as a consequence of which the corridors of economic power continue to extend in and around Whitehall. It is, therefore, all too clear that the student of Economics, whether he does so formally by taking it as a separate subject or not, is forced to concern himself with a study of the government of the country.

We think that, in a democratic society such as ours where the ultimate political power rests with the electors, much more effort should be made in schools to turn out pupils who are politically literate. Boys and girls should leave school with at least an outline knowledge of the basis of the political processes in the controlling of which they are destined to take an active and knowledgeable part, certainly as voters and perhaps many of them as workers or officials in national and local services. Yet how many of the youngsters who leave our schools have received any such opportunity to gain this knowledge? In the equivalent of our sixth forms in many American high schools the two subjects which are compulsory are Economics and the Government of the United States. Similarly pupils studying for the Baccalauréat in France are obliged to follow a course entitled 'Knowledge of the Contemporary World' which includes the evolution and workings of the French constitution.

The sixth-form course

Most of those who take British Constitution at school probably do so as part of a two-year sixth-form course and it is important that the teacher should allocate his time carefully and should decide whether or not he is going to cover the syllabus twice in these two years, or work steadily through it once. The subject does naturally fall into two parts: (1) the description of existing institutions, and (2) the critical discussion of the working of those institutions and an investigation of the alternatives. It is very desirable to have an understanding of the whole system of government before starting serious criticism of any part of it, since there is so much interlocking of the parts. On the other hand to teach the description without the criticism is equally undesirable, since it is likely to produce conformists whose reaction is to recoil from all change. In the main the 'O' level papers place more emphasis on descriptive knowledge while at 'A' level the emphasis moves to the ability to criticise. For the boy intending to take 'A' level, therefore, it works very well to take the 'O' level examination at the end of the lower sixth year and then go on to a deeper critical appraisal of the subject. Teachers would be making a big mistake, however, if they regarded the 'O' level course as being a purely descriptive one, as G.C.E. examiners look for critical comments and award marks for this extra information. The stereotype answer, for example, on the duties of a back-bench M.P. can be brought to life by pointing out ways in which more use could be made of their talents and, perhaps, by making comparisons with other countries such as the United States where a system of Congressional Committees can give real power to Congressmen who would only get it under the British system by attaining ministerial rank. In most cases your pupils will not have taken British Constitution at 'O' level at 16 and thus the 'O' level examination will be taken in the sixth form where already they will be adopting a more critical approach to their studies. Since, therefore, your candidates are going on beyond 'O' level with their studies it is important to put a larger critical content into the course than the 'O' level syllabus calls

119

for, so that your pupils do not get the impression that they are learning about a definitive and changeless system.

In the course of even a single year it is certain that some parts of the constitution will change and it is useful to deal with such changes at some length in order to bring out the evolving nature of the constitution. For example, it is regarded that Mr Callaghan left the Chancellorship in 1968 because of devaluation which was regarded as an admission of the lack of success of orthodox fiscal and monetary policy. This is in accordance with the normal idea of ministerial responsibility, that a minister should accept the consequences of the success or failure of his policy, but then why did he take another cabinet post as Home Secretary? The question of cabinet responsibility could be illustrated by Mr Cousin's resignation in 1966 because of his unwillingness to support the incomes policy. He could only stay in the cabinet so long as he supported government policy and resigned when he could not, in order that cabinet unanimity might be maintained. But how would your pupils account for Mr Brown's resignation in 1968 on the principle that cabinet unanimity was not being followed and that votes had been taken? The subject matter of the constitution is always changing and it is important that your pupils are aware of it. Many changes occur so rapidly that textbooks are made inaccurate between the time of writing and sale. The teacher must make note of these changes and should point them out to his pupils. Some of the changes are far-reaching and detailed and would necessitate the reading of White Papers, or at least press summaries of them, so that, for example, your pupils may know that, in the consideration of the Finance Bill, the House of Commons Supply and Ways and Means Committees have on occasion been replaced by Select Committees. There is nothing worse than for a teacher to mention something, perhaps on the basis of notes made a year or two ago, and to be corrected by a pupil who may have read of the reform in the press or seen it on television. Your pupils expect you to know these things, and although it is right to admit ignorance it is wrong to glory in it.

In this connection what has been said elsewhere in this book about keeping a newscuttings book is particularly applicable to the study of government. So rapidly does the subject change that you will probably find it necessary in your own interest to build up a card index, noting the major recommendations of royal commissions,

120

fresh legislation and new interpretations of law in the courts. You should urge your pupils to read the 'quality' newspapers and the informed weeklies, and if your own school library does not take these then you should make every effort to remedy the situation. Encourage your pupils to watch the political programmes on T.V. – 'Panorama,' 'The Week in Westminster' – and to listen to 'Yesterday in Parliament' on the radio for fifteen minutes every morning or the weekly summaries on Saturdays. It would make a welcome change from Radio 1! The teacher of British Constitution is fortunate in that there is such an *embarras de richesse* of printed information and much of this is worth keeping in its entirety, perhaps in the form of a scrapbook or else folded and slipped into envelopes and used as a card index with the subject name written on the tag of each envelope.

Visits

What has been said elsewhere in the book about visits applies equally to the study of government. You can help to bring your subject alive. by visits to Parliament, to your local council meetings, to the various courts of law, to the local Ministry of Labour employment exchange or to the offices of the Ministry of Social Security. All such visits will need careful planning and the value of the exercise will rest very largely on the way in which the visit has been preceded by teaching in class and on the way it is followed up afterwards. The visit should not just be an enjoyable afternoon out of school but it must be integrated carefully with what has been taught and what your pupils have read.

Just what visits are practical will depend upon where the school is situated. Londoners are fortunate in this respect, being at the centre of government and administration, and visits which last an afternoon, an evening or a whole day can be easily arranged. But Parliament is not very distant for many parts of the country given the vastly improved forms of communication. Manchester is only two and a half hours away by train, while Newcastle-upon-Tyne is only four. The latter is less than an hour away if an aeroplane is chartered. There is, however, no reason why a two- or three-day educational visit to the capital should not include both Houses of Parliament, the Law Courts, a tour of the Whitehall area and the London County Council, with Westminster Abbey and St Paul's included as cultural bonuses. If you are visiting the capital from outside you can always arrange to lobby your own M.P., and he will usually respond favourably and may perhaps act as your guide on your tour of the Houses of Parliament.

As far as local government is concerned no teacher can plead geographical distance as an obstacle to his visits. County towns are usually well placed for meetings of county councils and, if they are Assize towns, will probably have the whole range of courts, excepting only the Court of Appeal and the House of Lords. Remember that pupils visiting courts must be over sixteen years of age. But even if you do not live near a county town, or a county borough, local government still goes on and can be seen in urban and rural district councils and even the parish. For these latter meetings you do not even need to arrange formal visits. Suggest that instead of an essay for homework one week, two of your pupils visit the local council meeting, note its procedures and the business discussed and report on this, perhaps by reading a paper, to your class as a whole. Some teachers may hesitate at this but your pupils are old enough and responsible enough to do things without your supervision. It would pay you to be in touch with the town clerk's office so that you may be advised in advance of important meetings, especially of administrative tribunals which are also open to the public.

We feel that visits to places of political business are important, if only to stress the difference between the description of an institution in textbooks and how it works in practice. From the reading of a textbook your pupils might get the impression that the House of Commons is full of members all listening carefully to what is being said and then rushing out to vote on a matter. It frequently comes as a surprise when a pupil sees the chamber at work and finds it remarkably empty, with perhaps one or two cabinet ministers present and a person on his feet addressing the speaker who is, in the meantime, listening to a person dressed in an historical costume who is whispering in his ear. It is only when matters of vital importance are being discussed that the chamber is crowded, and on such occasions school parties cannot get access; what they do see on a normal visit is the routine of the day-to-day business of governing the country, which is remarkably dull and unspectacular to watch. Similarly a visit to the House of Lords would show the real power of that chamber by the fact that often there are only ten people in it. The same is true of local government. There is a story of a north country teacher whose pupil complained that the council meeting which he had attended was over in ten minutes; it was only when he met a councillor afterwards that the pupil was told that the real business had all been discussed in committee and all the Council was doing was giving its official approval. In the case of visits to law courts your pupils may well be surprised at the number of people who plead guilty by letter and do not even bother to attend the hearing of their own cases in the magistrates courts.

Just as visits outside school are important to your pupils, so are visits by outsiders to your school and you may even find it easier to obtain speakers on political affairs than to find speakers on economic affairs. Your local Member of Parliament is a busy person and has many claims on his time but you should be able to get him to address the school provided you give plenty of notice. Local politicians are generally much more easily obtainable since many of them are likely to have connections with your school; some of the school governors may be local councillors appointed by the council. These local connections need cultivating, but once matured they generally prove very fruitful and a visiting speaker may well suggest another person to you who would be only too pleased to talk to your class. Trade union speakers too generally give stimulating talks to your group and many pupils have been surprised at the difference between the quiet and highly responsible person addressing them and the excitable person shouting through a megaphone at a group of workers which is too often the image of the unionist on television. As one visiting trade union official said to a class, 'Our job is not to go on strike. Our job is to avoid this whenever possible and only use it as the last resort when all else fails.' This same speaker, an U.S.D.A.W. official, caused considerable amusement when he said he spent a great deal of his time seeing that shop assistants had adequate toilet facilities; in other words the regular routine is unspectacular and because of this seldom gets reported. It is very often only the person who is actually involved who can give the inside view, and this is of enormous benefit to your pupils.

Classroom methods

We said, earlier on in this chapter, that in the main we considered that the approaches to the teaching of Economics and to the teaching of British Constitution were similar, but that there were certain fundamental differences. We stressed that British Constitution is a subject which necessitates considerable amounts of reading and it is our view that the more reading is done, and the wider the sources of information and opinion on which your pupils can draw, the more benefits will they obtain. To what extent will your own teaching techniques be different from those used in teaching Economics? There can be similarities between the blackboard approach to dealing with the organisation of Parliament or the legal system and the organisation of the National Coal Board or of a large firm. There is no corresponding similarity to the geometric approach to teaching the theory of the firm. In this respect British Constitution differs very much from Economics in that its presentation is entirely a literary one, more akin to the presentation of History than Economics, whereas the latter uses some techniques that are more akin to Mathematics. It is important therefore that your pupils should acquire a literary outlook early on, and learn to marshall their thoughts and present them clearly in essay form.

In your own teaching of British Constitution you may well find yourself using a traditional 'talk and chalk' approach, but we would urge that this was not carried too far. Important points, such as the basic principles behind cabinet responsibility, can be prepared before your lesson and duplicated for handing to your class. Then, provided that your class has done its reading, and you should be urging it to do so, your lesson can become much more of the discussion type, with the teacher stimulating discussion and steering it along the right lines. At the end of your lesson you can sum up and write the salient points on the board for your pupils to enlarge upon by their own note taking. Thankfully your subject changes so rapidly that it is difficult to get into the rut of repeating the same information and therefore your pupils would not run the risk, as did one young master returning to teach at the school where he was once a pupil, of hearing next door his former History teacher giving exactly the same lesson as when he was a pupil, beginning with 'Congress of Vienna, Point One, England's attitude was . . .'. We feel that, when your pupils have gained a considerable amount of knowledge from their own reading your lessons can become discussions rather than formal 'talks' and we fully support the practice of one member of this panel who has dispensed with desks in his upper sixth classrooms and has his class sitting in armchairs and so gains a relaxed atmosphere which is conducive to discussion.

We do not wish to stress excessively the use of discussion as a teaching method, since so many other methods are at your disposal. You can make use of tape recordings of political broadcasts; you can listen to programmes about government which are included in the B.B.C. broadcasts to schools; and you can watch television programmes on the same subject. Why not, as a change from routine, follow the passage of a bill through Parliament by using Hansard? It may be that you choose to follow something of great importance like the Iron and Steel Nationalisation Bill, the discussions on which occupy many pages of reports on the deliberations of both Houses, or it might be something very small like the Bogglethwaite District Sewage Bill, on which only one person, namely the honourable member for Bogglethwaite, had anything to say. If you have not got Hansard at your disposal you can still follow the passage of a bill in the press, where papers like *The Guardian* give notice of Parliamentary business each day. Similarly you can make use of White Papers, reports of Royal Commissions, or evidence submitted by local authorities on matters which concern them. In the case of the latter the recent question of reform of local government caused most local authorities to submit detailed suggestions as evidence, in the course of which many large boroughs argued forcibly for the extension of their area whilst smaller ones opposed moves as a result of which they would lose their identity. Reports of this nature are invariably printed and can be obtained from the town clerk's offices. You could also profitably spend a lesson looking at published minutes of local council meetings, including important committees. The work of the education committee generally makes interesting reading, particularly if your pupils can read sometimes of a committee motion approving the paying of their grants to university, or approving a grant to help pay the cost of a school visit abroad.

As has been suggested above with regard to teaching Economics, considerable use can be made of case studies. Why, for example, in 1968 did Dame Irene Ward take the exceptional step of causing her own expulsion from the chamber? Was this personal or was some much deeper motive involved, including a protest against the swamping of Parliament by the government? If the latter is true, can your pupils suggest the reasons for this and could they suggest any alternatives. Has the British system so much legislation to deal with that we need a system of committees like the American ones – a division of labour within the Houses of Parliament? You could take the case of the resignation of Mr Brown in 1968 from the cabinet as an indication of a fundamental change in cabinet procedure. Does it indicate a break with the old idea of collective responsibility and cabinet unanimity? Is the election of a Scottish Nationalist M.P. a real sign that nationalism is a force of importance within the United Kingdom and is there a need for a greater delegation of powers to regions, with perhaps even regional government? If Ulster can have a separate Parliament within the Union, why not Scotland and Wales?

You can also make use of the occasional debate or partisan discussion as another teaching method. By allowing them to take sides, emotion can be used to provide fuel for the engine of reason. There are plenty of subjects to disagree about; the reform of the House of Lords, the case for the monarchy and electoral reform are hardy annuals, but are new to each generation of pupils. The thorough investigation of a specific problem, such as local reorganisation of secondary education, can usefully cut right across the conventional division of the subject, bringing in not only local government but the central administration, cabinet policy, Parliament and the testing of the law in the courts.

Books and written work

We have repeatedly stressed that we regard wide reading as being important, and the teacher today is fortunate in having a large number of textbooks available for school use. We mention some of them in the appendix at the end of this book. It is still true, however, that there is no perfect textbook, and the ideal is to have available sets of three or four different books, each of which will have its own special merits. The boy who relied on one book only would be not only a poor scholar but a dull one and the same would equally be true of the teacher.

As well as textbooks, a subject library is even more necessary than it is in the case of most other subjects. The boys should be taught not only to use the books for reference, but should also be guided as to which are the valuable parts of books to use, when the reading of the whole would make excessive demands on their time. Besides textbooks your pupils can gain an enormous amount of knowledge from the reading of political biographies. A book like Harold Nicholson's *Life of George V* is not only a model of what a biography should be but also throws fascinating sidelights on the function of the Monarch (especially the first few pages of chapter 5, and chapter 8). A pupil reading, at the beginning of chapter 5, the future King's own notes on Bagehot's famous chapters on the monarchy may well be stimulated to read those chapters in the original. And if your pupil does read those two chapters of Bagehot you will have put him on nodding terms with the classics. So make sure that your library contains these also, including the great works of political philosophy from Plato to Marx and Laski. One book leads to another. Not many pupils will read right through Dicey, but they could be encouraged to reach a chapter or two, if for no other reason than to see how lucidly and unambiguously different abstract ideas can be expressed – an example of style they might do well to emulate. Quite apart from the content of the subject, we shall not have wasted their time if, with us, they learn to communicate the kind of ideas that they might want to express later to company boards, or in civil service minutes, or even in drawing up a working constitution for a local football club.

At the 'A' level stage much of the reading will be an expression of a point of view and will inevitably be subjective. It is obviously desirable for them to read as widely as possible to balance the points of view. For example, Herbert Morrison's *Government and Parliament*, excellent as it is, needs balancing from a different standpoint, as, indeed does Harold Laski's *Reflections on the Constitution*. Thus, however modest your departmental library, it is essential that the books together present a balanced picture of the governmental processes. A book such as H. V. Wiseman's *Parliament and the Executive* is particularly useful since it contains selections from a great many writers representing a range of viewpoints.

We also feel that the student of political affairs can widen his viewpoint by the reading of works of fiction, just as can the student of History. There is a considerable fund of political fiction – Trollope's *Phineas Finn*, Bennett's *Lord Rainge*, Maurice Edelmann's *No love for Johnny* and Howard Spring's *Fame is the Spur* – all concerned with national politics, whilst Winifred Holtby's excellent

127

tale *South Riding* gives a well-informed picture of government at local levels. You can also use novels to illustrate foreign systems of government by recommending the reading of such books as Allen Drury's *Advise and Consent* – an excellent study of Congress as seen through the eyes of the minority leader, or Robert Travers' *Hornstein's Boy*, which describes in detail how a small-town lawyer gets elected to a midwestern state legislature.

'A' level British Constitution

In a large number of cases you will be pioneering this subject and you will be left very much to your own devices. It is up to you to decide what books to order and how to tackle the syllabus which is given to you by the examining boards. You must decide whether to go quickly through the syllabus in one year and revise it in the next, or to revise as you go along and take the whole two years to cover it. You must decide what essays you should set and how frequently. We have stressed that British Constitution is a literary subject and therefore considerable importance should be attached to written work. What we have said on this subject already about writing essays in Economics applies equally in this subject. You will find that past examination papers are of enormous help in showing what examiners expect your pupils to know and you should make use of these in your essay programmes which you set your pupils.

Remember that you must train your pupils to think, to understand and eventually to criticise the institutions of British Government, the structure of which is never static. Therefore you yourself must be aware of change and of the implication and significance of political events.

It is hardly likely, though it is not impossible, that your pupils will become cabinet ministers, M.P.'s or permanent under-secretaries. However, some may become local politicians or civil servants of various kinds. The majority will take work where their only contact with political matters comes at election times. But if your ex-pupils know of their own significance within the constitution, of their rights and privileges and of their responsibilities, and of the fact that it is they who ultimately govern the country, then your teaching will have served an invaluable purpose.

General Studies

The study of government is admirably suited for sixth formers as part of a General Studies course as although they are not going to sit an examination in the subject they are usually interested in politics. Modern sixth formers are much more alive to government than were previous generations. They want to participate more in the management of school or university because they are genuinely interested in behaving democratically. They have been found to be almost passionately interested in listening to political theory expounded and then discussing it enthusiastically and intelligently. British Constitution lends itself to discussion because it is so obviously a live topic and its functioning can be seen around us all the time.

The close links between British Constitution and Economics which are important to the 'A' level candidate are also relevant to the General Studies course. Students should have the opportunity to learn that the frontier between the economy of a country and its politics is a narrow one and sometimes there does not seem to be any barrier at all.

The psychological nature of politics need not be an insurmountable difficulty. The sixth former is intelligent and if he is interested, he is quite capable of understanding difficult ideas if he is introduced to them appropriately. He can be fascinated by the ambivalence of the private interest and the public interest. His own experience has already acquainted him with the powerful motive of self-interest, the need to do well in his examination. His participation in games and the prefectorial system, the timetable and private study, school uniform and tutorial idiosyncrasies, have informed him about the problems of individual liberty and the need for discipline both in a collective and a personal form, the necessity of a social spirit – or if you like, a team spirit. There is every reason to be optimistic and to issue a challenge to the student. He must discover that there are tensions in life, that his own wish to be autonomous, to establish an identity, will be furthered if he knows the sort of society into which he is about to be plunged, no longer sheltered by his parents or his teachers.

The teacher is recommended to read Professor Bernard Crick's essay in the Bulletin of the General Studies Association, no. 12,

TEACHING OF ECONOMICS IN SECONDARY SCHOOLS

Winter 1968, and *The Teaching of Politics*, edited by Mr Derek Heater.

A suggested course of General Studies in Government

The course which follows is designed to be covered in twenty forty-minute periods in one term and it is assumed that the course is part of General Studies and is not examinable. The class should however be asked to write two essays, one half-way through and the other at the end of the course. The class should be encouraged to read the 'quality' newspapers and journals, to listen to or view broadcasts on urgent public problems. The method recommended is a short introduction to the question to be discussed followed by a debate in which the teacher must lead in order to ensure that time is not wasted. It is wise to give notice of topics well in advance so that the class can think about them and come prepared with points to make and questions to ask.

Lesson 1 (or Period 1) should be an historical account of how human societies have been formed; man is a social animal, he likes company, he wants someone to talk to, he finds that living with other men is to the mutual benefit of all both in earning a livelihood through division of labour and in protection; the biological urge to live with a woman and start a family which grows into an extended family and then into a clan, a tribe, a city and a nation.

Lessons 2 and 3 should bring out the need for organisation and order because of the conflict between the private and the public interest. The customs and traditions of the community develop into laws which must be administered by courts and police and public opinion, which need to be revised and amended and repealed by a legislature.

Lessons 4 and 5 should discuss how this legislature is chosen, leading to the introduction of political ideas, like oligarchy and democracy, dictatorship or anarchy. What does democracy imply? Government by consent? The will of the majority? A universal franchise? Freedom of speech? Separation of powers?

Lessons 6, 7 and 8 can be a comparison between the philosophies of conservatism and liberalism, socialism and communism. All have virtues and all have weaknesses. Can there be a perfect system?

Lessons 9, 10 and 11 should be a discussion of British parliamentary democracy. What reforms are needed? Is the vote at eighteen a good thing? Is proportional representation feasible? Is the monarchy an anachronism? Should Scotland and Wales have an independent parliament? If the United Kingdom joins the Common Market, will this raise a question of sovereignty? The field of choice is almost infinitely wide.

Lessons 12 and 13 can be a discussion of public opinion such as demonstrations in Trafalgar Square or marches to Aldermaston. If Mr Enoch Powell comes down to speak, should he be given a fair hearing or should he be mobbed? Do party broadcasts on television influence voters? Should the Prime Minister be sternly interviewed or should he be allowed to see the questions he is going to be asked and choose the interviewer? Should the B.B.C. make jokes about the Prime Minister or the Leader of the Opposition? The existence of public opinion in the school should be raised, a topic with immense possibilities.

Lesson 14 could be a discussion of the mid-course essay.

Lesson 15 might be concerned with public control over people like publishers or theatrical impresarios, school teachers or university professors, newspaper editors or policemen. Is this desirable? Is it practicable?

Lesson 17 could be a discussion of the aims of government; is it the health and happiness of the greatest number? Is a materialistic attitude bad? Should church and state be linked or separate?

Lesson 18 ought to be an examination of local government. The class might visit the town hall; they should certainly know what the local authority does, how funds are raised, how they are spent, how councillors are elected, how the voters can influence them or communicate with them. The apathy and ignorance of local government is tragic and something has got to be done to persuade people to take more interest in local affairs.

Lessons 19 and 20 can be a review of all that has been done, giving the class the opportunities to raise questions that have been worrying them or points on which they are not clear. They might be given a reading list in the hope that they will continue to be interested in politics.

9

TEACHING AIDS AND ACTIVITIES

There is an apocryphal story of a teacher of many years' standing who believed that the most forceful and effective of visual aids was himself. His habit was to write sketchily and illegibly on the bottom corner of the blackboard without moving from his desk. When asked by one boy, 'Sir, what is that on the blackboard?' he replied, 'Mainly chalk.'

Teachers of Economics are generally cast in a less conservative mould, and are happy to evolve and to experiment with new ideas in teaching methods. *Economics*, the journal of the Economics Association, illustrates this concern, with regular articles discussing ways in which economic information may be disseminated. Because Economics is a relatively new school subject, teaching methods are relatively new, fluid and in a process of constant evolution. There is no accepted method of teaching the subject. The very nature of Economics releases the teacher from the bonds of tradition and encourages him to make use of new methods of presenting economic information in an efficient and interesting way. In this chapter we have gathered together information about teaching aids and methods of which we have personal experience and which we hope you will find useful so that you in turn will experiment and will devise still more successful methods. The chapter is divided into three parts: the first deals with audio-visual aids, the second with teaching activities and aids inside the classroom, and the third with various activities which may be organised outside the classroom.

Audio-visual aids

There is an immense literature on this subject. Two useful books are R. Cable, *Audio Visual Handbook* (U.L.P.) and L. S. Powell, *A Guide to the Use of Visual Aids*. R. H. Ryba's contribution to *Teaching Economics* (Economics Association) should also be noted.

TEACHING AIDS AND ACTIVITIES

THE BLACKBOARD DIAGRAM

For practical purposes, the blackboard or one of the newer types of chalkboard is likely to be our chief teaching aid for many years to come. At the outset we would emphasise the importance of using it effectively. Diagrams are a vital part of any textbook and the blackboard diagram is similarly important in the exposition of a great deal of theoretical Economics and its applications. Diagrams must be clearly and boldly drawn and correctly labelled: you cannot expect your students to draw neat graphs, with the point of origin, the cost and output axes clearly shown and cost curves appropriately marked *ATC, AVC, MC*, as the case may be, if your own work has been hurried or careless in this respect.

Blackboard illustrations may be used to make clear, for example, the relationship between a number of financial institutions, or to illustrate the principle of the division of labour, or the concept of the circular flow of income. Many of these may be adapted from textbooks and in this connection we would specially recommend you to study the diagrams in Harvey's *Elementary Economics* and *Intermediate Economics*, and Marshall's *Comprehensive Economics*. Others you will be able to design yourself; you will soon discover whether they clarify the point you want to make or make it more difficult for your class to grasp. We include examples of both the blackboard summary and the graphical explanation types of diagram.

Equilibrium positions

COMPETITIVE INDUSTRY

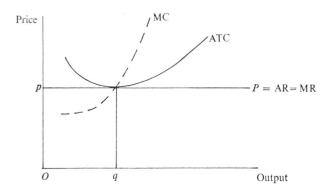

133

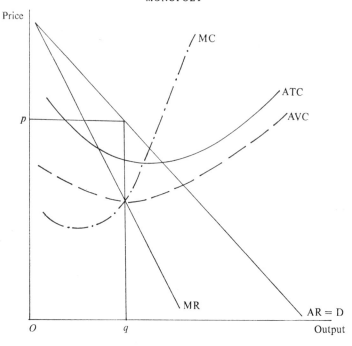

The use of a bill of exchange

Rolls Royce
(Producer)

Delivery of cars worth £1 million
──────────────────────────────────→
+ Bill for acceptance

Henlys
(Distributor)

Return of accepted bill
←──────────────────────────────────

Rolls Royce take bill
to be discounted

Barclays Bank
(or discount house, etc.)

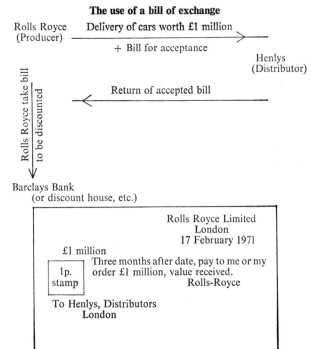

Rolls Royce Limited
London
17 February 1971

£1 million

1p.
stamp

Three months after date, pay to me or my
order £1 million, value received.
Rolls-Royce

To Henlys, Distributors
London

Discount rate: 5% e.g.

TEACHING AIDS AND ACTIVITIES

Division of labour

1. *Simple division* – one man – one 'complete' job

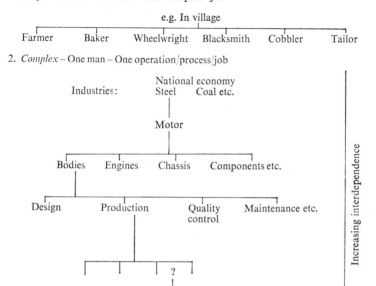

2. *Complex* – One man – One operation/process/job

The development of specialisation

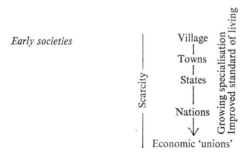

Prepare your diagrams beforehand as part of your teaching notes, but it is a mistake to put them on the blackboard before the lesson begins. The great advantage of the blackboard over the textbook illustration or wall-chart is that it allows a diagram (perhaps a very

135

complicated one) to be built up step by step in a series of easy stages. If you are describing the Bank of England and open-market operations you might begin with the simple diagram below:

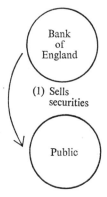

A discussion of the way in which the Bank sells securities to the public, which will probably be through a financial institution, and the effect of these sales on the commercial banks would follow. The public will draw cheques on the commercial banks in favour of the Bank of England and the cash balances of the former will fall:

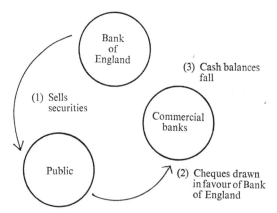

There would follow an explanation of the reactions of the commercial banks following a fall in their cash balances. Their response would be to call in loans to the discount houses who would be forced to apply for help to the Bank of England. The Bank will always assist the discount houses, but only on its own terms, and if these are penal terms there will be a general upward movement of short-term interest rates:

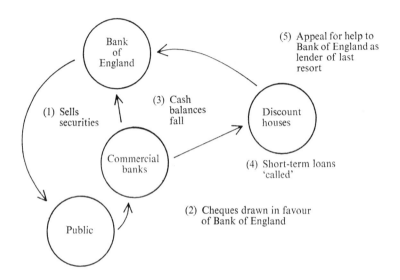

This is quite a complicated diagram, which would cause confusion if a class were confronted with it at the beginning of a lesson, but which they can grasp if gradually built up step by step – if needs be, during a succession of lessons.

The full relationships are too complicated to show adequately but the original diagram may be built up still further to show the structure of British financial institutions and the flow of funds between them, the Treasury, and the public. The purpose of such a diagram is to illustrate the fact that there is a complexity of financial institutions which are interconnected by a complicated flow of loans and debts. With this diagram you could point out, for example, that when open-market operations force the commercial banks to 'call' in money from the discount houses, these latter are still supplied with funds from the overseas and foreign banks. You could point out, by referring to this diagram that, because of the complexity of the flow of funds, traditional monetary policy is not as effective is it used to be.

137

British financial institutions: Flow of funds

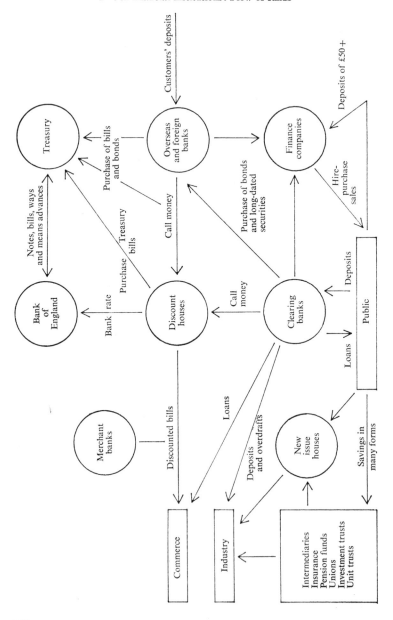

Another vital function of the blackboard is to help your class to understand the type of diagrams encountered when dealing with the theory of price or the theory of the firm. In the early stages of many Economics courses a high proportion of boys and girls are confused by the simplest of demand and supply diagrams. To the teacher, diagrams are a familiar and useful way of expressing certain concepts; they are alternatives to verbal explanations, just as to the mathematical economist the same concepts may be stated with precision and brevity by means of equations or formulae. A class beginning to study economic theory is not familiar with such diagrams and it is easy for the teacher to forget this. You may assume that the class can readily interpret a sloping demand curve as another form of the statement 'As the price of a commodity falls, the demand for it increases'. In fact, the class will often grasp the verbal statement readily, while having greater difficulty in understanding the diagram which you think is making your meaning clear.

We suggest you proceed cautiously at this stage, explaining to your class that you are introducing them to diagrams as an alternative to what might be lengthy or clumsy verbal statements. For instance, you should write up the demand schedule to show how the demand curve is derived from this. Try to detect and to check any tendency on their part to assume that economic theory is in some mysterious way a theory about diagrams. You will find traces of this misconception when they write; 'The equilibrium price is the point where the demand and supply curves intersect', or when they assert; 'The entrepreneur's profit will be maximised when his marginal cost curve cuts his marginal revenue curve'.

Once the class has begun to grasp the idea of the diagram as an alternative means of expressing economic relationships and one which will help them to deal with certain problems very quickly and conveniently, the blackboard becomes exceedingly useful. When dealing with, for example, the theory of the firm, the writer of a textbook is limited by reasons of space in the number of illustrations he can provide. With a blackboard the teacher is not handicapped in this way and can draw as many diagrams as necessary. The first, perhaps, will show the firm's average variable cost curve and the second the firm's average fixed cost curve. In each case you will need to explain that the graph also shows the firm's total variable

139

or fixed costs at any given output. Your third diagram will bring these two cost curves together as an average total cost curve with the average variable cost curve shown, perhaps, in a contrasting coloured chalk. Finally, the marginal cost curve is drawn and its relationship to the average variable and average total cost curves explained. Total cost at a given output may be derived from the average total cost curve. No textbook can afford sufficient space for diagrams on this scale; in this respect you are superior to the most accomplished author and we feel that the blackboard is, and is likely to remain, of great value.

OVERHEAD PROJECTORS

Much of what we have said about blackboard work applies to the overhead projector as well. The projector is a glass writing-desk with a strong light beneath it. A diagram, a statistical table or, for that matter, anything that would normally be written on a blackboard is drawn on a transparent sheet of acetate or an acetate roll and the image is projected by means of a focusing lens on to a screen above and behind the teacher's head.

Transparencies of diagrams from books and magazines may be made with a photocopier or heat copier, but you can easily make your own diagrams using a spirit-based felt-tip or fibre-tipped pen. By superimposing transparencies simple diagrams may be built up into more complex ones; using outline maps and a series of overlays such topics as the changing location of industry may be effectively illustrated.

The projector is a versatile piece of equipment and, in using it, you have the advantage of facing the class during the whole of your lesson as well as avoiding the inconvenience of chalk dust. You will be able to prepare much of your illustrative material beforehand. On the other hand, effective use of a projector requires a certain degree of skill and, until they have had experience in its use, many teachers find it less flexible than the blackboard.

WALL DIAGRAMS AND CHARTS

Diagrams and charts on stout paper may be permanent records of work done on the blackboard or projector in lesson time, or may be more elaborate affairs using pictorial material. Some of these you will probably prefer to make for yourself to achieve that precise degree of elaboration – or simplification – you feel is needed. A chart showing the structure of some large firm, illustrating horizontal and vertical integration, diversification, holding companies and subsidiaries, is often useful; so too are charts showing the development of the existing machinery for investigating monopolies and restrictive practices, or the relationship of the Treasury, the Board of Trade, the D.E.A., and other government departments involved in economic affairs.

Some excellent wall-charts are available from such bodies as the Bank Information Service, the Iron and Steel Federation and several large firms. Details of these are given in the bibliography. Whether you use these professionally produced charts or make your own, it is wise policy to display them for strictly limited periods of time – a fortnight or three weeks at the most. If left on display for any length of time they will come to be ignored and will fail to make any effective impact on your class.

THE 16-mm FILM PROJECTOR

Most schools will possess a 16-mm projector which can be used in a darkened room with a screen of suitable size. This is a useful visual aid, but the extent to which you will use it will depend to a considerable extent on how easily you are able to overcome a number of practical difficulties. The blackout must be efficient or picture quality will suffer. The projector is a complex and delicate piece of equipment – some training is needed to be able to use it without risk of damaging it or the film. In practice many teachers find it difficult to erect a screen and a loudspeaker and to operate a projector without losing a great deal of time at the beginning of the lesson. The National Committee for Audio-Visual Aids publish a handbook on *Film Projecting* which is very helpful in this respect.

It is an advantage for the teacher to see the film before showing it to the class and it is important for him to allow sufficient time before the film for an introductory briefing and for a follow-up discussion afterwards. A major difficulty in using films is that the teacher has to accept what the film-maker has produced. He cannot be selective, cutting out those pieces of film he considers irrelevant or badly done, or extending some valuable scene. He cannot replace

141

the commentary, which can be irritatingly technical or ludicrously childish and over-simplified, though the film may be visually excellent. While many of the films issued by firms or organisations such as the Stock Exchange Council are of interest to economists, few of them have been made for teaching purposes but there are still sufficient which are both useful and relevant to the Economics lesson for the teacher to make it worth his while to master the techniques of film projection.

Films are often useful as introductions to a particular topic, or as summaries; they do not replace the teacher but only reinforce his teaching; they are teaching aids, not teaching methods. A list of film libraries containing films which may be useful to an Economics teacher is given in Appendix II.

THE 35-mm FILMSTRIP PROJECTOR

Some of the difficulties involved in using the 16-mm film projector apply to the use of the 35-mm filmstrip projector, although the latter is relatively easier to use. The only warning necessary is that if the projector does not have an efficient cooling fan care must be taken not to project a single frame of the filmstrip for too long a period or the film will burn.

Filmstrips are generally produced specifically for teaching purposes. The Economics Association, for example, has prepared filmstrips on *The Location of Industry in Great Britain* and *The Retail Trade*. There is not a great number of filmstrips on aspects of Economics, though mention may be made of *Samuelson's Economics*, produced by McGraw Hill, *An Introduction to Economics* by Common Ground, and *Basic Economics* by Encyclopaedia Brittanica. There are, however, many filmstrips containing material which is useful for background or introductory purposes, particularly in recent economic history. Examples of these are *Coal Mining* and *Iron and Steel*, both by Common Ground, *Twentieth-Century Britain* by Educational Publications and *The National Budget* by Pitmans.

Some filmstrips have been prepared as part of a 'teaching kit', together with booklets and wall charts. These are designed for C.S.E. and 'O' level G.C.E. classes, and the banking and building societies study kits produced by Educational Productions Ltd are strongly recommended.

Each teacher will of course discover very quickly how much use he wishes to make of these aids and the techniques he uses to present a topic with a good degree of visual impact will depend upon many factors. You should guard against the blunting of your enthusiasm for visual techniques by irritating administrative difficulties that are beyond your control. If, to obtain the use of a room with an effective blackout, the movement of other classes from their usual rooms must be undertaken you will not find it easy to show films – but these administrative difficulties should not blind you to the improvement in your teaching which could result from the use of these techniques. If you really believe that visual aids have an important place in your Economics teaching then none of the difficulties are insurmountable. Whether you find visual aids useful depends in large measure upon your energy in preparation, but the use of well-prepared aids often brings handsome rewards in the depth of understanding, interest and enthusiasm of your pupils.

Classroom activities and aids

When you start to teach Economics to a class you will probably find that most of them regard it, as they regard other school subjects, as something that happens just within the four walls of the school. You will probably find too that most of them do not regularly read the newspapers or watch news items on television. If they do, they will probably pay little attention to the items which interest us. One of your first tasks is to persuade them that in studying any of the social sciences they are not learning about remote things, things which happened hundreds of years ago or thousands of miles away. They are trying to understand what people are doing all around them; you have to show them that this is one of the most fascinating of pursuits. How can you do this? Turning from the complicated and expensive devices discussed in the previous section, you can encourage them to read the newspapers systematically, to learn what people are doing and from this it is only a short step for them to provide their own teaching aids.

NEWS CUTTINGS BOOKS

From the start it is a great help if you are able to illustrate your lessons from current events. Composite demand seems less of an academic exercise when it is seen to relate to a piece in the newspaper about the price of men's shoes being affected by the fashion among women for boots which use more leather. With a combination of luck and good management it is possible to arrange things so that the teacher is dealing with public finance at budget time or has just covered foreign exchanges when the government decides to devalue. Having acquired the attitude that what is talked about in school is linked with what is happening outside, the class can be encouraged to look for their own examples to illustrate the theories they have studied. It is now that the news cuttings book comes in, and they can be asked to clip out and paste in to it relevant items which they have found for themselves in the newspapers and journals. It is important that all the cuttings pasted in their books are related to the subject dealt with in school. They should, therefore, be made to cross index their cuttings book with their notes. In this way, two useful objectives are achieved. They begin to look around for examples to illustrate principles, and they, also, begin to analyse events from an economic viewpoint.

Of course we do not want to make a burden of the news cuttings book, but an occasional look at them and a word of praise for the good ones will help a lot. The offer of a small prize at the end of the year for the best, human nature being what it is, may help even more. An alternative to this, at sixth-form level, is to compile cuttings books on specialist topics. One member of the form may be responsible for up-to-date news and articles on the balance of payments; another, on the work of the Industrial Reorganisation Commission and so on. These cuttings books can be kept readily available in the Economics room.

CASE STUDIES

The use of case studies as a method of teaching Economics is a fairly recent development arising from their use in business schools. So far their use has been confined to supplementing and developing the student's ideas and understanding of specific topics.

The actual case study takes a variety of forms. It can for example, be a study in depth of a particular firm which illustrates specific and identifiable features. Alternatively it can be a quantitative example based on real data selected to illuminate the topic. Much

144

interesting work is going on in this field and the Economics Association is planning to produce a series of books based on case studies.

Role playing is a method of encouraging students to use their imagination to deal with specific problems. This method has also been developed by business management schools in recent years, but experiments are being made in developing and adapting it for use in schools.

Students enjoy 'acting out' situations that involve portraying the actual or supposed actions and ideas of people. They identify themselves easily with the character and situation of the person whose role they are playing and, very often, through play, the whole group benefits from a transfer of learning. An exercise of this kind may involve you in a great deal of preparation in the first instance, but can be very rewarding.

At quite an elementary level, to bring home the complexity of the financial world and to introduce the class to the basic concept of choice, there is that old favourite, the £10,000 legacy. If you were suddenly told that you had inherited £10,000, and assuming you were not going to spend it immediately, how would you dispose of it?

Some members of the class, suitably briefed, can take the parts of possible recipients of the legacy: the owner of a small business; a young man about to marry; a widow with young children; a retired person drawing a pension, and so on. They can apply for advice to representatives of, say, a building society, a unit trust, a stockbroker, a bank manager or an official in the National Savings movement. There can be a third group who will discuss among themselves the merit of the advice given, and help the recipients of the legacy to decide on their courses of action.

All those who take part must be given sufficient time to prepare themselves for their parts. Explain the scheme to your class, and allot them their roles well in advance.

We have worked out in detail the following example of role playing used with a sixth form after about a term's Economics. A few days before the exercise each member of the class was given a duplicated sheet containing the following information and volunteers

145

were called for to play the main parts. This gave them a chance to find out in advance as much as they could about their subject and the characters they were playing.

SNOW CLEARING ON THE ROADS

Object of the exercise: to bring out the differences between the technical and economic aspects of a problem.

Meeting of the Highways Committee of the Blankshire County Council

Agenda

1. To discuss the dislocation on the roads caused by the recent snowstorm.
2. Steps to be taken for the future.

Present

> Chairman of the Committee
> County Surveyor
> County Engineer
> County Treasurer
> Members of the Highways Committee

Basic information

1. *Blankshire*

   (a) *Roads*

Class A roads	242 miles
Class B roads	417 miles
Minor roads	1,365 miles

   (b) *Finance*

Rateable value	£9 million
Product of penny rate	£37,000

2. *The officers*

   The County Surveyor: Responsible for the roads – has 50 men under him – on the defensive.

   The County Engineer: Brought in to advise on equipment – keen on change – wants more mechanisation.

   The County Treasurer: Concerned with cost – the economic adviser.

The need for snowploughs, more grit lorries, tons of salt and much more temporary labour was stressed and it became clear that, if enough money was spent, the county need never again be disrupted for a week by snow as it had been. This is where the treasurer came in, to point out that other things would have to be cut down to pay for it all . . . and a discussion of choice and alternatives foregone was under way.

An essential part of the exercise is the discussion afterwards. This ranged over other situations posing similar problems – a recent railways accident at an automatic level-crossing which could have been avoided at the cost of manning all the gates – an elderly patient suffering with kidney disease who could be kept alive at the cost of a kidney machine and constant medical attention . . . and so on.

It is important in role playing that all taking part see the relevance in what they are doing. Topicality is a great help. The snow-clearing exercise was prompted by a nation-wide snowstorm a fortnight earlier. It was a bonus that on the day following the exercise we learnt that a nearby local authority had discussed the same matter on the same day. They decided to authorise the payment of telephone charges in the home of all those employees who might need to be called out. This was a technical, and economic, factor that even our surveyor had not thought of.

The particular study had an additional value to the class since they were also studying British Constitution. It gave them a chance to identify themselves with local officials and a local committee and to realise a few of the problems facing a local authority.

Role playing lends itself very effectively to the problems of private enterprise. It takes time to make its point, but it does make it firmly. Here are some general suggestions which may help you in developing your own ideas:

Casting

The roles that boys are to play as members of a business enterprise should be carefully defined. Whether they are fourteen or eighteen, boys have little concept of the role that businessmen play. The fact that the managing director rides in a chauffeur-driven Bentley whilst the apprentice rides a motor-cycle with a noisy silencer suggests much more to the average fifth former about the relative status of these two people than is or can be suggested by our examination of modern techniques of decision-taking on the pyramid of managerial responsibility in the running of a business enterprise. So, in allotting the parts that the pupils are to play, you should give a finely drawn picture of the work and responsibility of the businessman, privately and in detail to the boy concerned, and in summary to the class as a whole.

147

Supporting cast and 'Walk-on' parts

Everybody in the class should have some role to fulfil. With a small group there is no problem in this respect; each of the boys may become a director of the firm and the operation of the enterprise may be assumed to be entirely a result of the board's deliberations. If the class is a large one a business problem could be chosen which involves discussions and decision-taking at several different levels within the structure of the firm. It may begin with a meeting of several shop-stewards, resulting in a delegation to the works or personnel manager, followed by a series of meetings of the works joint consultation committee to which the area organiser of the trade union is invited. This would be followed by a report to the board of directors and so on. Everyone in the class should have a role to play.

The actor-manager

Once the initial preparations have been made including all the arrangements for 'stage management', the teacher should become just another member of the group. You should not remain aloof from the proceedings, neither should you make comments from the sidelines. You should play a role in the enterprise which is certainly not one of the major roles, such as chairman of the board, and is probably a role that nobody else wants. Once you have assumed this role you should ignore all but the most desperate cries for help and must ignore all appeals which would give you additional task of umpire – 'He can't do that, can he, Sir?'

Stage management

Before the drama begins every preparation should be made to create a realistic atmosphere. Arrange the room to look as much like a board-room as possible. The tables or desks can be arranged to give some impression of a conference table or it may be possible, in some cases, to use the school library. The company secretary ought to be able to provide everyone with a couple of sheets of notepaper, a freshly sharpened pencil and maybe even a glass of water. The sales and production directors could be encouraged to prepare production and sales charts which could be pinned to the wall or demonstrated on the overhead projector. How far the teacher and the class decide to go in these matters is obviously their own decision.

148

The choice of play

Careful consideration must be given to the selection of the business problem to be solved. At least for the first 'game' the teacher should select the problem. If the class should prove very proficient at the game it may, later, start to introduce its own problems but there are enough difficulties at the outset to warrant the teacher's choice of problem.

(i) The problem should be a simple one which is part of the day-to-day running of an enterprise – it won't be a routine problem to the class.

(ii) The problem must be capable of solution – and a fairly straight-forward solution – by the particular group of boys. It is pointless to start off with a discussion of the best way to relate manpower planning to capital investment programmes.

(iii) A full briefing on all the relevant factors that may enter into the discussion including the fullest possible appreciation of the situation must be given to all the class.

Various problems can be introduced such as:

(i) The discussion following a report by the sales director of a falling off in either national sales or the sales in a particular region.

(ii) The discussion about problems likely to be met when changing from hourly rates to piece rates of payment for factory workers.

(iii) The problems of introducing a new sales campaign.

(iv) The problems posed by a piece of government legislation and what steps the firm can take to solve them.

(v) The problems posed by devaluation.

(vi) A discussion about whether shareholders should be advised to accept a take-over bid for their shares made by a rival firm.

(vii) The problems of redundancy due to the introduction of more advanced technological methods of production.

These problems are advanced in what may be regarded as ascending order, according to the probable complexity of their solutions and according to the number of problems which they pose.

'First night'

The first meetings of the board may well prove to be disastrous. One possibility is that no-one will say anything, no decisions will

149

be taken and the problem will remain unsolved. It is here that the teacher encounters his chief danger. Understandably distraught at the waste of your time, enthusiasm and careful preparation, you will tend to leap into the fray and try to force the directors to a decision and some sort of solution. Unless you have already decided to abandon the technique as yet another of those experiments that didn't work, you ought to restrain yourself. The ploy here is to prepare a 'news item', to be read out the next day, reporting the collapse of the firm and the forthcoming trial of the directors on charges of fraudulent conversion, negligence, and whatever else comes to mind.

On the other hand the first attempt may reveal one or two cases of incipient and hitherto unsuspected megalomania. Then the enterprise may become a one-man show, in which case the teacher should immediately arrange a take-over bid by an insuperably powerful rival firm.

What it really amounts to is that the first attempt should be regarded as a trial run. As the pupils become more accustomed to their roles, which should not be changed once they have been decided; as they begin to realise that fulfilling their role is a demanding affair; as they talk among themselves about the firm and their own place within the firm the whole experiment will take on both a serious and a successful air. The problems discussed will become more complex, the solutions to them more reasonable and the decisions taken more ingenious as time goes on.

PROGRAMMED LEARNING

A different way of involving the individual pupil more deeply in the topic under consideration, is that of programmed learning. There is a considerable literature on this method of teaching, and mention should be made of H. Kay, B. Dodd and M. Sime, *Teaching Machines and Programmed Instruction* (Pelican); G. O. M. Leith, *Handbook of Programmed Learning* (Educational Review Occasional Publications); or you may prefer to begin by teaching yourself, using, for example, the International Labour Organisation's *How to Read a Balance Sheet* (I.L.O., Geneva).

Programmed learning – using specially designed books or the more elaborate teaching machines – may be used in many different ways. You may find it useful in breaking up the routine of formal teaching, or to reinforce some topic which the class seems to have found difficult. You may find it useful for revision purposes, or for helping a boy who has been absent for some time and has missed a good deal of work. Enthusiasts for programmed learning would claim that it often makes more efficient use of the teacher's time, allowing him perhaps to teach larger classes successfully. It gives each member of the class the opportunity to work at his own pace; it continually demands a response from the student and the learning process is constantly reinforced and tested. Within limits, the speed of learning seems to increase.

A number of programmed texts on economic topics are available, and a number are quoted by P. S. Noble in her contribution to *Teaching Economics*. You will probably want to write your own to fit the particular requirements of your class or your course. We would suggest that you proceed cautiously here, selecting topics which are as self-contained as possible and which can be dealt with in a short programme.

Suppose, for example, that you have discussed exports, imports, the balance of trade and the terms 'favourable' and 'unfavourable' when applied to the balance of trade. You may have dealt with these terms in quite a general way, and now wish:

(a) to reinforce the class's grasp of the terms;
(b) to test the class's understanding of terms;
(c) to extend the class's knowledge of Britain's own balance of trade.

You might then give each member of the class duplicated sheets and encourage them to work at their own pace through the following questions, appealing to you if any difficulties are encountered. These are not programmed learning, but are a useful method of testing the topic.

BRITAIN'S BALANCE OF TRADE

Fill in the missing words. Ask for help if you have any queries.

1. The 'balance of trade' of a country is the difference between the value of the country's exports of goods and the value of its imports of goods over a period of time – say, a year. It is sometimes called the country's *visible balance*.

A country's visible balance is the difference between the value of its exports and the value of its . . . .

2. When the value of a country's exports is *greater* than the value of its

151

imports, there is a *surplus* of exports over imports. A trade surplus occurs when the value of . . . . exceeds the value of a country's . . . .

3. Britain had small trade surpluses in 1956 and 1958. In these years the value of Britain's exports . . . . the value of Britain's imports.

4. The value of Britain's exports exceeded the value of her imports (that is, she had a trade surplus) in the years . . . . and . . . .

5. Another term which may be used to describe a trade surplus is to say that the balance of trade (or visible balance) is *favourable*. When the balance of trade is favourable, the value of . . . . exceeds the value of . . . .

6. We can say that in 1956 and 1958 Britain's visible balance was . . . . or that there was a . . . . on her balance of trade.

7. When the value of a country's exports is not as great as the value of her imports, the balance of trade is said to be *unfavourable*. An unfavourable balance of trade occurs when the value of imports . . . . that of exports.

8. Other terms used to describe an unfavourable balance of trade are *trade deficit* or *trade gap*. A trade deficit occurs when the value of . . . . exceeds that of . . . .

9. For more than a century the annual value of Britain's imports has nearly always been greater than the value of her exports. For over a century, therefore, Britain's balance of trade has nearly always been . . . .

10. For more than a century, Britain's balance of trade has nearly always been unfavourable. Another way of describing Britain's trade position would be to say that there has generally been a . . . . on her balance of trade.

11. In 1965 the value of Britain's exports was £4,784m. and the value of her imports £5,053m. In this year, Britain had a . . . . on her balance of trade.

12. The deficit on Britain's balance of trade in 1965 was £269m. (The difference between £4,784m. and £5,053m.) Another way of describing Britain's trade position in 1965 would be to say that she had an . . . . balance of trade of £269m.

13. In 1966 the value of Britain's exports was £5,116m. and the value of her imports £5,222m. Because the value of her imports exceeded the value of her exports, we can say that in 1966 Britain had a trade . . . .

14. In 1966 Britain imported more goods (by value) than she exported, and had a trade deficit of £ . . . . m.

15. In 1966 Britain had a trade deficit of £106m. As compared with 1965 the size of her trade deficit was . . . .

16. In 1967 Britain's trade deficit was £552m. The value of Britain's exports in that year was £5,023m.; the value of her imports was £ . . . . m.

17. The size of Britain's balance of trade fluctuates; the balance is usually unfavourable, but in . . . . and . . . . there were small trade surpluses. In 1965 she had a deficit of £ . . . . m., in 1966 a deficit of £ . . . . m., and in 1967 a deficit of £ . . . . m. This means that in 1967, for example, the value of Britain's imports . . . . the value of her exports by £ . . . . m., and the trade gap was . . . . as big as it had been in 1966.

This is not intended to be an example of a programmed text which in any case would be arranged and printed in a more elaborate form. These questions apply the principles of programmed learning to class teaching purposes and illustrate the way in which a short exercise may be prepared. In this example each question demands a one-word answer and care has been taken to avoid confusion as to the word required: the topic is unusually complicated in that a variety of terms – 'trade gap ', 'trade deficit', 'unfavourable visible balance' and so on – are in common use to describe the same situation.

In preparing a piece of work of this kind – or in making copies of extracts from books or newspapers, statistical material or diagrams – a spirit duplicator is an invaluable aid. This machine will produce large numbers of copies from a master sheet on which material has been typed, written or drawn. Diagrams in several colours may be produced, and the master sheets filed away for future use. An enormous amount of time may be saved by using this machine and its versatility would lead many teachers to consider it their most important single aid.

TAPE-RECORDERS

Most schools now possess a tape-recorder, and this too can be a useful teaching aid in the classroom. The recording of radio broadcasts of lectures and discussions and to a limited extent of television broadcasts can provide stimulating material for class discussions. A few years ago recordings were made of J. K. Galbraith's Reith Lectures; these were played back to a class which was already familiar with his writing and its members were further stimulated by the breadth of his vision and observation. It was a very useful exercise because the class not only heard and were stimulated by something they would normally have missed but because they listened to it together as a group in the context of a formal lesson. Student Recordings supply a whole range of pre-recorded tapes covering a wide range of topics in Economics. Also, J. Weston's *The Tape Recorder in the Classroom*, published by the National Committee for Audio-Visual Aids in Education, contains advice on setting up a tape-recorder and on suitable teaching techniques.

Tape-recorders can also be used to record class discussions. Where discussions emerge spontaneously and are pursued vigorously by the class it is helpful if you can allow them to develop without interruption. Later, when the recordings are played back, the main points may be summarised and an effort made to reach some general conclusions. A further benefit from the tape recorder is that it is possible to link up work in different classes. For instance, a good discussion from a previous year may be played to a class as a starting point for further discussion. Similarly a lower sixth class may be used to prepare a detailed piece of research incorporating recent developments which may be played to an upper sixth class for revision purposes.

You are sometimes at quite short notice required to be away from a lesson. When that happens, you can arrange to play a recording of an important topic which can later be discussed by you and the class who will have made notes about the talk they have heard in your absence. This is a most useful device.

Teaching aids outside the classroom

We have constantly emphasised in this book the special character of Economics in that it can appeal to boys and girls much more than other academic subjects because it deals with 'real life'. In case studies and role playing we encourage them to identify themselves with situations which might occur in the adult world. We can go still further in this direction by leaving the classroom and taking classes into the world of industry, or by inviting outside speakers to address Economics Societies.

WORKS VISITS

Works visits are designed to let your classes see how goods are actually made and what 'labour' and 'capital' look like on the factory floor.

Before the visit

Begin by writing to firms at least six months ahead. Many firms have a long waiting list for visits and cannot arrange them at short notice. Explain that you want to bring a party to visit the works, say whether they are boys or girls, give the approximate size of the party, and make it clear that they are studying Economics. State the average age of the group, and indicate whether they are 'O' or 'A' level students. Let the firm know what dates would be convenient to you and ask them to arrange for a party. Most local authorities require such visits to be formally approved, so check on local regulations as well as obtaining your headmaster's consent.

154

There may be comparatively few factories in your neighbourhood or an embarrassingly large number. Make enquiries of other Economics teachers in your area; senior members of staff, the parent-teachers' association secretary and the local youth employment officer can all be helpful with suggestions and possibly with introductions. How many visits you arrange is for you to decide. Begin with one a term, or possibly two contrasting visits within a fortnight of each other in each of the first and second years.

If you have some choice of visits, try to choose at least one example of mass production methods which use flow-line assembly and extreme division of labour in a works which is capital intensive and which shows marked technical economies of scale. Or you might prefer to make the contrast between a firm which is mainly concerned with assembling a finishing product and one which starts off with basic raw materials and processes them. This point about contrasted firms is important; much of what pupils will see in their first visit will acquire a much greater significance when they make their second visit and see a quite different range of processes, differently organised.

When the visit has been arranged, make sure that everyone concerned is told the time and date well in advance. Contact the firm two or three days in advance and check that they are expecting you; make a point of asking how big a party they can take. The firm may restrict the size of your party to twenty or twenty-four. This may be because they intend to provide several guides who will each take charge of a small group. Beware of the firm that invites you to bring as many as you like; you will probably find that the party is assigned to a single bashful apprentice who is too shy to speak and who can't be heard anyway.

In the week before your visit brief your class. Point out that the factory is organised to produce goods, not to entertain visitors. Your visit will almost certainly add to the firm's costs of production. Point out that floors can be greasy and machinery so placed that casual strolling round in large groups is impossible. Above all, it will be noisy, much noisier than they expect. Sometimes guides are equipped with hand microphones but invariably an extra effort is needed if everyone in the party is to keep up with the guide's commentary. Guides are human and are bored by parties who are indifferent to what they say; they appreciate the parties which show interest and ask questions.

155

The more information and guidance you can give your boys and girls before they enter the factory, the more they are likely to notice and to understand. Sometimes the firm will send a brochure which will give some indication of what the party will see: often a remarkable amount of information about an industry, simply expressed, is easily accessible in volumes VII and VIII of the *Oxford Junior Encyclopaedia*.

The visit

Make sure that everyone has a small notebook and a duplicated sheet of points to look for. You may draw up this list of questions with a particular firm in mind, or you may prepare one of more general application. Here is an example of the latter, drawn up for a party from a second year sixth:

Works visit: Try to find out the answers to these questions.

1. *Ownership and control of the firm*

    Public or private company?
    Shareholders – widely distributed or large family or institutional holdings? Foreign control?
    Sources of new capital for expansion?
    Subsidiary of larger firm, or itself controlling other firms? Association with other firms in horizontal or vertical combine?
    Relation of firm to industry? Degree of competition within the industry – monopoly or oligopoly?

2. *Location*

    Dominant factors influencing location? Raw materials, power, labour, transport factors? External economies? An example of geographical inertia?

3. *Costs of production*

    Sources of raw materials? Power and heat requirements? Water needs and supplies? Skilled/unskilled labour requirements? Recruitment and training of labour? Labour or capital intensive?
    Fixed and variable cost ratio? Effect of increases in individual costs on total costs? Important content of product?

4. *Production techniques*

    Nature of production – largely assembly of components, or processing of basic materials?
    Range of processes? Integration of processes? Diversification of product? Type and range of products?

5. *Scale of production*

    Examples of division of labour, flow production, automation? Are there further opportunities for economies of scale? Any conflict between technical and marketing optima?

Difficulties or ease of altering level of output? Elasticity of supply of firm's products?

6. *Markets*

Outlets for products? Proportion of output which is exported? Consumer or capital goods market? Branded product? Price fixing? Price discrimination? Sales promotion? Advertising policy? Elasticity of demand for product?

There are many other questions which could be raised – how decisions on pricing and output are made, for example – but the average school party will be lucky if it meets anyone sufficiently well-informed to answer this type of question. Your students will not get answers to all the questions on this list but it will prompt them to think, look and ask.

After the visit

Your follow-up to the visit is also important. Discuss the main points listed in your questionnaire; ask the class what they found was interesting and most significant. Do not be disappointed if the response is poor after the first visit; the novelty of the works, the noise, heat, smell are often overwhelming and leave little but a very confused impression. Even when sons of colliers go down a pit for the first time they tend to be quite unprepared for what they see and feel.

A letter of thanks from the class will be appreciated – it will also make the personnel officer or whoever arranged your visit more sympathetic to future requests for visits.

Films, which we discussed earlier, are both alternatives and supplements to outside visits. In some areas, a film like *Project Spear* may be the only practical approach to the problems of the steel industry. To those who have visited a steel works, or indeed are going on such a visit, the film provides background information and a vivid impression of a capital intensive industry. Boys and girls can often assimilate this more easily than when they are overwhelmed by the heat and noise of an electric arc furnace.

Other visits

Many other visits can be arranged which will be of general interest and of particular value to Economics students. If you happen to live in London obvious examples are the Stock Exchange, the Bank of England and the Royal Mint. Visits to docks or a large bus depot can be rewarding.

157

A more ambitious scheme, but one which has been carried out successfully, is to arrange 'industrial tours', possibly at Easter or Whitsuntide. A group of sixth-form economists from, say, the London area, might stay a few days in the north of England and visit a coal mine, shipyard or textile mill; a party from the north might profitably spend a few days in London seeing something of its financial institutions at first hand, or a series of visits might be planned having a central theme, for example, public enterprises.

AN ECONOMICS SOCIETY

As an Economics sixth increases in size there is much to be said for the starting of an Economics Society. This should be open to all members of the upper school, since most intelligent young people are aware of, and interested in, economic affairs, even though they may not all be taking a formal course of study in them. A wide membership is also a useful recruiting device in that younger members of the school, say fifth formers, can have their interest stimulated, particularly if they do not come into contact with teachers of Economics during their lower school work.

An Economics Society should aim to stimulate the study of, and an interest in, all matters appertaining to Economics and associated subjects such as Politics and Economic History. A wide range of activities is possible, including addresses by visiting speakers, debates, film shows, visits to factories or public meetings, or even informal gatherings where general discussion over coffee can take place. We have stressed the importance of visiting speakers, and of outside visits to factories and financial institutions and there is no reason why these activities should not be organised under the auspices of an Economics Society. A visiting speaker may, for the same reason, prefer to address the Economics Society than the Economics sixth. The former title has a more attractive ring to it than the latter.

Since meetings generally take place after school hours it is useful to arrange for coffee and a light snack to either precede or follow the meeting, so that pupils can have some chance to meet the speaker more informally. Boys are sometimes shy of voicing opinions in public but may not hesitate when they see the speaker in less formal surroundings, balancing a saucer and cup of coffee in one hand and toying with a sandwich in the other. Contacts can also be made more easily by boys acting as officials of the Society. The teacher can say 'May I introduce John Green, Secretary of our Society, I believe you've had some correspondence'. This is preferable to a line up of sixth formers, as if they were film actors at a Royal Command Performance. If the Society is large in membership let the speaker have tea with the committee.

A debate, organised by the Society, is generally a popular activity in any school. The politicians are good targets and motions such as 'This house has no confidence in the economic policies of Her Majesty's Government', or else, 'This house rejects the government's strategy for the south-west', ought to stimulate a good attendance. If there is already a debating society in the school then offer to sponsor particular debates and provide speakers on subjects relevant to Economics; debating society chairmen will generally welcome such an offer.

The teacher should always be aware of activities and events concerned with the field of Economics taking place in his locality or region. Local authorities organise exhibitions on development projects; colleges organise one day conferences; factories have official openings; speakers of eminence give public addresses. Why not encourage your pupils to go informally to these things, say as individuals, or as groups? Let them act as delegates from the Economics Society, to report back to the full membership at formal meetings or even at a symposium.

It is important that the pupils should carry as much of the burden of running the Society as they can. A teacher may think that the job is more easily done if all the burden is carried by himself, but this is usually self-deception. Elect a committee and give it responsibility. Allow the secretary to do all the correspondence for the society, including the writing of letters of thanks to visiting speakers, or to public relations officers of firms who have organised industrial visits. Make sure that the treasurer keeps funds adequately – this latter may involve nothing more than collecting money for visits, or to pay for refreshments, but it is responsibility and generally pupils value this. Consult freely with your committee as to the society's programme of future activities. What visits would they like? If only one is allowed this term, shall it be a coal mine or a steel-works? Get them to suggest visiting speakers – often they have better

159

contacts than the teacher, particularly if he is a newcomer to an area. It is surprising how many good contacts can be made this way – the father who is a stockbroker, an uncle who is a trade union official, a friend of the family who works for the county planning department.

We feel that it is important that a subject should exist outside as well as inside the classroom. Economics, more than most other school subjects, is about real contemporary problems. A good Economics Society can help, by getting pupils outside the textbook and outside the classroom, and by bringing outsiders into it, to make the subject 'live'. If Economics is the 'core' of a group of subjects, then extend society activities to these – a Political Club for those reading British Constitution, an Industrial Archaeology Group for those reading Economic History. There is generally wide scope and the teacher should do all he can to utilise youthful enthusiasm which, all too often, in a good number of cases, remains untapped.

This chapter contains a great fund of practical advice on the teaching of Economics. Much of what we have said is idealistic and we accept this. We realise and are familiar with the practical difficulties involved in using many of the aids we have suggested. It is not only a question of money to purchase much of the equipment but also a question of time. The Economics master who has just finished taking a junior History or perhaps a Mathematics class in the lower school may find that he lacks the time to black out a room, set up a projector and erect a screen to show either slides or films during a short lesson. Hence we stress the value of ancillary staff to arrange these things for the teachers – technicians to prepare lessons involving visual aids, and clerical assistants to prepare charts or notes, say for a role-playing exercise. We also know that the running of extramural activities is time-consuming, and the demands of the Economics Society may well clash with the demands of the teacher's family. We realise, therefore, that considerable extra effort is required by the teacher who wishes to make use of the variety of aids and activities which are available to him. The ones we have suggested have all been used by the members of this committee and they will continue to be used since we are convinced that they are instrumental in improving the quality of our teaching.

10

THE FUTURE

It was a sunny morning in early May when Sherlock Holmes called me to the window of his sitting room at 122ʙ Baker Street.

'I think we are going to have a visitor, Watson,' he said. 'What do you make of the man standing by the flower-seller on the corner, yonder?'

'He is a man of about thirty-five,' I said. 'He is of medium height and build and appears at first sight to be in good health.'

'Yes, yes!' cried Holmes, a note of impatience entering his voice, 'but what is his occupation, my dear man – what do you judge him to be?'

I confessed myself baffled, and turned to Holmes for enlightenment.

'Tell me about his dress, Watson,' said Holmes.

'He is neatly but rather shabbily dressed,' I replied.

'Quite so, quite so,' said my friend, 'and it will not have escaped your notice that he is wearing the distinctive tie of one of our best known universities. The inference is clear enough. A graduate, yet badly paid; he cannot be employed in commerce or industry, where the services of suitably qualified graduates are in great demand and the remuneration notoriously high. He cannot be one of the professional men whose incomes are derived from fees and commissions and have kept pace with the rising tide of inflation. No, Watson, the situation is clear enough; indigence and intellectual ability are found today only in the Established Church and in the teaching profession. Our man has chalk dust on his lapels. His place until recently was in the classroom.'

I turned to Holmes in amazement.

'Astounding!' I cried, 'But surely that is all?'

Holmes drew me once again to the window.

'Observe him closely,' he said. 'Certain occupations produce easily identifiable physical changes in those who practise them. The stenographer's finger-tips are calloused; the acrobats of our music halls possess well developed pectorals and deltoids; our man down there has a slight droop of the right shoulder, a thickening of the elbow. It comes from his daily task of turning the handle of a spirit duplicator. Undoubtedly it is his duty to instruct the young in the principles of Political Economy.'

It may not be true that the Economics teacher spends more time than his colleagues in performing routine tasks; we feel, nevertheless, that in discussing the possibility of achieving greater efficiency among Economics teachers, we should draw attention to the need to free them from the burden of clerical work that could better be done by others. Indeed, there are other ways in which we feel that the standard of teaching in this subject might be raised by increasing the provision of teaching aids, not only of those already mentioned in this book, but also of more elaborate devices and by improving the skills of the individual teacher.

The increased provision of teaching aids

From time to time in this book we have drawn attention to the difficulties facing the teacher who is inadequately equipped. His first need will be sufficient textbooks and a library of more specialised texts. No teacher can be expected to work effectively unless he is freed from worries about the supply of books. As with the more elaborate teaching aids, projectors, tape recorders and so on, the problem here is essentially one of money. We have suggested that a variety of aids may be useful in teaching Economics. We would argue that the principle of increasing returns operates as additional units of equipment are applied to the fixed teacher-factor. We feel that the special needs and opportunities of the subject, rather than some crude calculation based on numbers taught, should be the basis for allocating capital expenditure.

We look forward to still more elaborate provision in the future. There is much to be said for specially designed and equipped teaching rooms for Economics, or for teaching units with classrooms, library, store and work-rooms adjoining. Such a room should be planned so that visual aids could easily be used; there would be ample wall space for the semi-permanent display of charts or diagrams and facilities for storing files, press cuttings books, pamphlets and bank reviews. Such a room might become something of a common room for all sixth formers studying Economics.

Another possibility is the use of closed-circuit television. In its simplest form, this would consist of a camera connected to monitor sets in one or more classrooms, if parallel classes were being taught. With this the teacher could prepare and give a lesson complete with diagrams, models, charts and any other visual material he considered necessary.

Visual material could be used in this way with the maximum effect giving the teacher the opportunity of producing a lesson unhampered by the physical limitations of classrooms that are too small or lacking in wall space. Educational use of video-tape recording equipment in this country is only just beginning, though much experimental work is being carried on. The possibilities here for increasing the productivity of the teacher are immense.

162

THE FUTURE

Secretarial and technical help

No matter how competent the teacher, or how well-equipped, his teaching abilities will be reduced if a considerable part of his time is taken up by clerical and routine work. The Crowther Report called for 'a realistic study of possible ancillary services of all kinds to save the teacher's scarcer skill' and it is taken for granted in universities and colleges of technology that secretarial help should be made available to staff.

Many of the techniques which we have described in this book place additional burdens on the teacher; the production of typed stencils, of multiple-choice questions, of programmes for teaching machines, of work sheets or assignments, of reading lists and examination papers – all these are time-consuming and are best left to be done by some suitably qualified assistant.

The tasks of duplicating material, of using a photo-copier to prepare transparencies for an overhead projector, of filing cuttings and looking after the Economics library, are other jobs which might with advantage be taken out of the hands of the Economics teacher.

The setting up of visual aids, their maintenance and their operation, are also time-consuming tasks. They often demand technical skills which the teacher lacks and are better done by an assistant. The principle of technical assistance of this type is well established in science departments, and we should press for the provision of the same help for the social sciences.

There is a strong economic argument for valuable and expensive teaching skill to be released from routine and less skilled tasks. The opportunity cost of typing and duplicating, when done by a qualified economist, is very high. The educational argument is stronger still. The teacher must be left with more time and energy to concentrate on his main task, that of developing to the full the intellectual abilities of his students.

Improvements in teaching skills

In spite of all that we have written about aids and equipment, Economics rooms and ancillary staff, the teacher's grasp of his subject and his competence to teach remain the most important factors of all. The quality of the teaching of Economics in some

163

schools has been criticised, and is one reason given by those university teachers who say they prefer their Economics students not to have taken it as a school subject. One of the principal objects of this book, of course, is to help to free the teaching of Economics from this type of criticism.

However, we feel that very much more could be done in other ways. In spite of the growing popularity of Economics as a school subject there are still very few colleges of education offering Economics as a main subject. In spite of the dramatic increase in the numbers of undergraduates studying Economics and of the growing numbers of Economics graduates entering the teaching profession, opportunities for graduates to receive specialist help from institutes of education are virtually non-existent. In this respect we hope our teacher training institutions will take steps to meet the challenge presented by the rapid growth of a new subject in our sixth forms.

It has been said that the major problem in teaching is that of keeping the boy at the end of the back row awake. Expensive equipment or duplicated material alike will make little impact if the class is unresponsive and the teacher lacking in enthusiasm. Throughout this book we have emphasised our belief in the importance of the personal qualities of the teacher. We hope that our colleagues, to whom the book is addressed, will benefit from the ideas and experience of those who have written it; we hope too that we shall all bring to the teaching of the subject energy and enthusiasm.

APPENDIX I

Bibliography in Economics

The aim of this bibliography is to provide the teacher, especially the new teacher, with a select list of books to think about and choose from; some of them may not suit him, others will. To help him in his deliberations we have made notes about each book. These are not in any way criticisms of any book, but remarks about contents, publishers, dates, some biographical notes about authors, all of which, we think, are useful to know. The list is not exhaustive, nor is it intended to be. The teacher will, if he joins the Economics Association, as he should do, obtain from them a much fuller bibliography of books about Economics. The catalogues published by the Economist Bookshop (at the London School of Economics, Houghton Street, London W.C.2) are comprehensive as well but do not quote publishers. Publishers are only too willing to send teachers information about their books and to provide inspection copies. This is a practical and inexpensive way of having a good look at books, getting the feel of them, and deciding whether they will suit your needs or not.

We have also included some information about journals and where to get them.

You are likely to be faced with the problem of the allocation of scarce resources between competing wants in a particularly difficult form in deciding which books to buy for class use. However big the class, you are unlikely to have enough money to buy all the books which you feel you need. Book allowances in most schools are based on the numbers taking the subject in the previous year, and a teacher who is introducing Economics to the curriculum, or is successfully enlarging a sixth-form group, may therefore find that needs for money continually outgrow the allocations, though probably this sad state of affairs is true of most of our activities.

How may the book allowance be best used? Elsewhere in this book it has been assumed that the fourth and fifth forms will have a standard textbook and you were advised to give each sixth former two or three textbooks and to provide a range of more advanced or more specialised books for reference. These may be counsels of perfection because to provide books for a class of fifteen or so students, at current prices, would require an outlay of about £75. Allocation of funds may well be on a more modest scale, especially in a school where the subject is new. Nevertheless you should do your best to persuade your headmaster to be generous.

Even if he is generous, you should still think hard about your books and buy wisely. Naturally opinions will differ on how to do this. Many experienced teachers believe that the provision of a standard textbook has the top priority. It will be prudent to remember that most textbooks are not written specifically for sixth formers, and that much will depend on the type of paper (or papers) set by the examining board with which your school is concerned. You will be fortunate if there is a single textbook which covers the course completely. It is also true in a field in which opinions are changing and new ideas being introduced, that a book becomes obsolescent far too quickly. One solution which works reasonably well is to buy a few copies of the latest edition of each of several standard textbooks each year. In this way you will usually have a decently up-to-

165

TEACHING OF ECONOMICS IN SECONDARY SCHOOLS

date stock of books and, unless your students are particularly destructive people, you will, in two or three years time, build up a reasonably adequate library.

ELEMENTARY ('O' LEVEL) TEXTS

Croome, H. and King, G. *The Livelihood of Man* (Chatto and Windus, 1963). Aimed at the 'O' level syllabus this book has a particularly good section of descriptive Economics.

Harvey, J. *Elementary Economics* (Macmillan, 1965). Covers all the ground necessary for an 'O' level syllabus.

Williams, G. *The Economics of Everyday Life* (Penguin, 1967). Written for the general reader, it serves as a good introduction to the subject for pupils below sixth-form level.

Stanlake, G. F. *Introductory Economics* (Longmans, 1967). A good 'O' level text, written by a schoolmaster, and is suitable for use at higher levels. Good diagrams but lacks chapter exercises. If the class is already provided with a simpler book it could be used as a second string for greater depth.

Harbury, C. D. *Descriptive Economics* (Pitman, 3rd ed., 1966). This is an excellent description of the U.K. economy. It is well set out, and contains plenty of statistics and diagrams, together with exercises at the end of each chapter.

Sladen, C. *Everyday Economics* (Pitman, 3rd ed., 1967). This is a simple approach for use up to C.S.E. and 'O' level, though it would need some supplementing. The style is readable and some interesting exercises based on newspaper extracts, as well as examination questions, are included.

ADVANCED LEVEL: BASIC TEXTS

Benemy, F. W. G. *Industry, Income and Investment* (Harraps, 2nd ed., 1967). Designed for both 'O' and 'A' level. It is a useful introduction to the subject and covers a wide area of ground from industry to macro-economics. Useful for lower sixth work.

Benham, F. (revised by F. W. Paish). *Economics* (Pitman, 8th ed., 1967). A popular and well established textbook which has been revised by Professor Paish and published under the title *Benham's Economics*. A clear style of presentation, and particularly useful as regards international economics and current planning problems.

Cairncross, A. *Introduction to Economics* (Butterworth, 5th ed., 1966). A first-rate description of economic problems and the orthodox solutions written by an authority on the subject. A very suitable sixth-form book with excellent sections on money and banking.

Edwards, G. J. *The Framework of Economics* (McGraw Hill, 1965).

Eastham, J. K. *An Introduction to Economic Analysis* (E.U.P., 1951).

Hanson, J. L. *A Textbook of Economics* (Macdonald and Evans, 3rd ed., 1961). A book now well established in Economics teaching and widely used for a variety of courses. Popular with most sixth-form students because of its simple presentation. Covers a wide area of ground, is well illustrated by diagrams and contains a useful selection of examination questions.

Harvey, J. *Intermediate Economics* (Macmillan, 1965). A very useful 'A' level text with progressive questions at the end of each chapter. The book is well written and contains a number of well constructed diagrams.

Nevin, E. J. *Textbook of Economic Analysis* (Macmillan, 3rd ed., 1967). A lucid presentation of the ground which needs to be covered in a course on Principles

166

of Economics. Sixth formers will need to complement this book by another on applied/descriptive Economics. A workbook, priced at five shillings, accompanies this text.

Marshall, B. V. *Comprehensive Economics* (Longmans, 1967). One of the newer textbooks which aims to cover all aspects of the subject, theory, applied and descriptive. Although a lengthy book, it is not longwinded and is easily understandable, being particularly well illustrated by diagrams. Contains a useful selection of examination questions at end of each chapter.

Lipsey, R. G. *Positive Economics* (Weidenfeld and Nicholson, 2nd ed., 1963). An excellent finishing book for the sixth former and should be in both the school and departmental library. Particularly fruitful on the theories of perfect competition and monopoly and on the circular flow of national income. Well illustrated by diagrams.

Pen, J. *Modern Economics* (Penguin, 1965). A very clear account of the important developments in macro-economic theory since Keynes. For the upper sixth and scholarship work.

Samuelson, P. *Economics* (McGraw Hill, 7th ed., 1967). A large and expensive book, particularly suitable for school and departmental library. Superbly produced with illuminating diagrams it is one of the best books of its kind. Most chapters contain a discussion of the application of theories, and the last section of the book discusses current problems of growth and economic policy. Accompanied by a workbook.

Speight, H. *Economics* (Methuen, 1961). Primarily a university undergraduate text, but suitable for sixth formers. The book concentrates on the relationship between theoretical and applied Economics.

Stonier, A. W. and Hague, D. C. *A Textbook of Economic Theory* (Longmans, 3rd ed., 1964). A difficult book for the sixth-form student but rewarding when the effort is made. An excellent discussion of employment theory and Keynesian Economics is included towards the end. For the library.

WORKBOOKS

Following a trend established in America some authors have published a work-book which can be used by the student to test his understanding of a text. For example, J. A. Stilwell and R. G. Lipsey's *Workbook* to accompany Lipsey's *Positive Economics* presents a series of exercises to test the understanding of each chapter. The answers are supplied and it is clear how they have been reached. A number of discussion questions follow and then a short summary, point by point, of the chapter. For the more able members of the second-year sixth, and for the teacher, this is a valuable book and will provide many ideas for adding variety and interest to the treatment of basic topics.

MORE SPECIALISED TEXTS

Brooman, F. S. *Macro-Economics* (Allen and Unwin, 2nd ed., 1963). Mainly used by second-year university students, but useful for reference purposes for the sixth-form student.

Dowsett, W. T. *Elementary Mathematics in Economics* (Pitman, 1959). Written for university students and covers the whole subject of Mathematics in so far as it is required for a study of economic principles and analysis.

Hansen, A. H. *A Guide to Keynes* (McGraw Hill, 1963). A very concise explanation of the ideas of Keynes which have had such an influence on subsequent economic thought.

Henry, S. G. B. *Elementary Mathematical Economics* (Routledge, Keegan Paul, 1969). A very simple and clear book which introduces the student to functions, graphs, calculus and other mathematical tools of economic analysis.

Hicks, J. R. *The Social Framework* (Oxford, 3rd ed., 1963). An excellent introduction to the study of national income flows, balance of payments and population problems.

Keynes, J. M. *General Theory of Interest, Employment and Money* (Papermac, 1963). Since this book has had more influence on economic thought in the twentieth century than any other, it deserves to be on your shelves and known to all your pupils.

Lekachman, R. *The Age of Keynes* (Penguin, 1967). Mainly for the library. Contains a readable account of Keynesian Economics, plus an account of the times and ideas in which Keynes lived, including his experience of the Versailles negotiations.

Phelps-Brown, E. H. and Wiseman, J. *A Course in Applied Economics* (Pitman) 2nd ed., 1964). Some parts of this book will be heavy going for most sixth-form students, but it contains excellent chapters on the problem of monopoly, the development of monopoly policy, and pricing policy for nationalised industry.

Ryan, W. J. L. *Price Theory* (Papermac, 1958). A university-standard book. Valuable to the sixth former in its discussion of monopolistic competition and price discrimination by monopolists. Also contains a clear account of indifference curves.

Robinson, E. A. C. *The Structure of Competitive Industry* (Nisbet, 1958) and *Monopoly* (Nisbet, 1941). Two small books in the Cambridge Handbook series which can be used by pupils who find basic texts too easy. It is not necessary for pupils to be familiar with all the theory in these books, but the descriptive passages are particularly useful.

INDUSTRY AND THE BRITISH ECONOMY

Allen, G. C. *The Structure of Industry in Britain* (Longmans). A study in economic change, discussing the causes and effects. Chapters 3 and 4 on restrictive practices are particularly useful.

British Industries and Their Organisation (Longmans, 2nd ed., 1966). A detailed account of the major industries in the British economy. Perhaps too detailed for basic texts but excellent for reference.

Donaldson, P. *Guide to the British Economy* (Penguin, 1965). This book makes a general survey of the major economic problems facing Britain, including industrial efficiency, the nationalised industries, the trade unions, monetary policy, taxation and sterling and the balance of payments.

Dunning, J. H. and Thomas, C. J. *British Industry* (Hutchinson, 1966). A clear account of the growth of British industry, containing much useful information in the form of both facts and figures. The subject matter is dealt with in general, rather than by studying individual industries.

Grove, J. W. *Government and Industry in Britain* (Longmans, 1967). This book discusses the role of the government as regulator, promoter (or entrepreneur), purchaser and employer. A mine of useful information for the school or departmental library.

Harrod, Sir R. *The British Economy* (McGraw Hill, 1963). A scholarly assessment of the monetary problems facing the British economy, particularly in the international field. An excellent reference book.

Lee, Anthony and Skuse. *Studies in the British Economy* (Heinemann, 1969). A very useful new series of handbooks, constantly brought up to date for 'A' and 'S' level pupils.

    Monopoly (1969). The first in the series covers the theory of monopoly and oligopoly, a survey of monopoly legislation and three case studies of oligopolistic market structures.

    Regional Planning and Location of Industry (1969).

    Britain's Overseas Trade (1969).

Livingstone, J. *Britain and the World Economy* (Penguin, 1969).

Marshall, B. V. *Comprehensive Economies* (Longmans, 1967). Already referred to as a basic text, part 1 of this book is full of excellent information on British industry, with major industries being studied at elementary and more advanced levels.

Prest, A. R. *A Manual of Applied Economics* (Weidenfeld and Nicholson, 1966). Contains good, up-to-date information on the current economic situation, but the book assumes a lot of background knowledge. For the library.

Sampson, A. *Anatomy of Britain Today* (Hodder and Stoughton, 1965). An account of how Britain works, who runs it and how they got there. It will provide a very entertaining account of the economic and political scene, whilst explaining the background against which Economics is studied.

Smith, G. *Britain's Economy* (Mills). A very useful book which confines itself mainly to the problems of home inflation and the balance of payments. Easily readable and can be understood by most pupils.

Shonfield, A. *British Economic Policy Since the War* (Penguin, 1958).

Tivey, L. *Nationalisation in British Industry* (Capes, 1966). A short account of the background to nationalisation which examines the attitudes of the political parties to the major controversies and discusses the problem of policy making. Contains useful information on the major nationalised industries.

Turner, G. *The Car Makers* (Penguin, 1963). A very readable history of the British car industry which describes the growth of a typical 'heavy' industry in which the technical division of labour has been used deeply and widely.

Worswick and Ady. *The British Economy in the Fifties* (O.U.P., 1962). Successor to their previous book *The British Economy 1945–50*, it traces the development of the economy during the fifties and discusses the major problems encountered.

H.M.S.O., *Britain, An Official Handbook*. This book is revised and re-issued every year. It contains accounts of all the major aspects of the economy, including population, industry, agriculture, the social service and government. Excellent reference material.

MONEY, MONETARY POLICY, FINANCE, BANKING

Brittain, S. *The Treasury under the Tories 1951–64* (Penguin, 1965). The first part of this book contains an excellent description of the organisation of the Treasury, a fundamental British economic institution.

Day, A. C. L. *The Economics of Money* (Oxford, 1963). This book covers most matters relating to money, from its origins, the development of banking and the problem of monetary policy. Very valuable section on international monetary problems.

Einzig, P. *Monetary Policy, Ends and Means* (Penguin, 1967). A clear statement of contemporary government policy and aims by one of the most informed commentators on this subject.

Ferris, P. *The City* (Penguin, 1960). A most entertaining and knowledgeable account of the City of London, discussing such things as take-overs and generally expanding on items which are treated in simple form in most textbooks.

Morgan, E. V. *A History of Money* (Penguin, 1965). A well established and highly readable text which traces the evolution of money in all its uses.

Robertson, Sir D. *Money* (C.U.P./Nisbet, 1948). Both an entertaining and evocative book. It is specially good on the rate of interest and is written from a different angle to the Keynesian approach.

Sayers, R. S. *Modern Banking* (Oxford, 7th ed., 1967). A standard classic in its field, elegantly written and easily readable. Frequently revised and up to date it is particularly useful on the topic of central banking.

H.M.S.O. *The Committee on the Working of the Monetary System* (1959). Reports of this nature come out only once every thirty years and are of major significance. Useful for reference, both for detail of matter discussed and for showing pupils how governments try to understand major economic problems.

Clarke, W. M. *The City in the World Economy* (Penguin, 1967). This book contains an excellent account of the City's markets in capital, commodities, shipping and insurance. There is also a good discussion of international liquidity.

Crowther, G. *An Outline of Money* (Nelson, 2nd ed., 1948). A well established text which traces the origins of money and enlarges on to the banking and monetary systems. For the school or departmental library.

ADDITIONAL TEXTS: INTERNATIONAL, TAXATION, FINANCE, HISTORY

Barber, W. J. *A History of Economic Thought* (Penguin, 1967). A useful background study to economics, dealing with the classical, Marxist, neo-classical and Keynesian schools of thought. Discusses the work of the economic thinkers in the light of their own times.

Beveridge, Lord W. *Full Employment in a Free Society* (Allen and Unwin, 1960). A good example of the role of the economist in the real world. It is now of historical interest to see the pre-war problems and the solutions produced. The prologue to the latest edition, 'Sixteen Years Later' is worth recommending on its own as an expert's essay on the question, 'Is inflation the price we pay for full employment?'

Deane, Phyllis. *The First Industrial Revolution* (C.U.P., 1965). A well documented discussion of the Industrial Revolution, its causes and effects, which gives the reader a clear picture of the evolution of the modern industrial economy.

Estall, R. C. *Industrial Activity and Economic Geography* (Hutchinson, 1966). A study of the influence at work in the concentration of industry geographically.

Galbraith, J. K. *American Capitalism* (Penguin, 1957). This book, a best seller, attacks obsolescent thinking about the creation of demand by advertising, etc. Has many interesting observations on production in the U.S.A.

The Great Crash (Penguin). An account of the Wall Street slump, its casino-type atmosphere, its effects on the world economy. In a sense the book is a severe criticism of the get-rich-quick mentality.

Harrod, Sir R. *International Economics* (Nisbet/C.U.P., revised ed., 1958). A very readable discussion of the theory of trade, the balance of payments and international monetary problems.

170

Hicks, Ursula. *Public Finance* (Nisbet/C.U.P., 1951). The fullest academic discussion on taxes and budgets at present available. Hard going for most sixth formers but useful for the library.

Kelsall, R. K. *Population* (Longmans, 1967). An up-to-date discussion of the influences determining the size of a population, with particular reference to the U.K.

Kenen, P. B. *International Economics* (Prentice-Hall, 2nd ed., 1967). An American publication which discusses the theory and application of this part of Economics. The book contains a very good outline of the problems facing the reserve currency countries, and assesses the development of international economic co-operation.

Lewis, W. A. *Theory of Economic Growth* (Allen and Unwin, 1955). Very good for scholarship work or pupils intending to study Economics at university. It is an interesting way of putting Economics into perspective with other subjects, and the literary philosophical approach may appeal to sixth formers studying arts subjects but not Economics.

Robinson, Joan. *Economic Philosophy* (Penguin, 1962). Mrs Robinson points out, in this book, that values ought not to be measured in terms of money alone. Particularly useful on the question of development and underdevelopment.

Roll, E. *The History of Economic Thought* (Faber, 3rd ed., 1964). A book for scholarship and upper sixth use. It traces the development of economic thought from the Greeks to modern times.

Sandford, C. *Taxation* (I.E.A. Key Discussion Book 4, 1966). A good account of the British taxation system, giving particular stress to some of the newer taxes such as capital gains and S.E.T.

Tew, J. B. *International Monetary Co-operation 1945–67* (Hutchinson, 1967). A good account of the evolution of the international payments system including discussion of the institutions evolved in the post-war period.

Selected books on British Constitution

British Constitution may appear also under the guise of Government or Political Affairs, since different examining boards use different titles. The list which follows is by no means complete. You are advised to watch the newspapers and, if the reviews of a book attract you, to ask the publishers to send you an inspection copy. You will in any case be sent notices of books by the publishers and the school will be visited regularly by their representatives. There is a vast literature on this subject and you will have no difficulty in suggesting titles for the school library.

BASIC TEXTS

Harvey, J. and Bather, L. *The British Constitution* (Macmillan, 1968). As its title implies this is a textbook expressly designed for the G.C.E. syllabus. It is very popular and covers the ground in one volume.

Benemy, F. W. G. *Whitehall – Townhall* (1967), *The Elected Monarch* (1965), *The Queen Reigns* (1963) (Harrap). These three books are designed to cover the ground both for 'O' and 'A' level G.C.E.

Powell-Smith, V. and Barber, P. *British Constitution Note Book* (Butterworth). This little book aims to help the student's memory. It has the merits of being concise, factual, accurate and up to date. It has the demerit that it can tempt the lazy to learn it by rote and to neglect their general reading.

Bagehot, Walter. *The English Constitution* (Oxford Classics) with an introduction by A. J. Balfour, or Fontana Paperbook (Collins) with an introduction by R. H. S. Crossman. Although this book was first published in 1867 it is still well worth reading as an introduction.

Mosley, R. K. *British Constitution 1968–69* (published by the author at 8 Cedar Avenue, Southampton, 1969). This little book deals with the developments in the constitution which have occurred during the year, and gives recent examples to illustrate other constitutional features. It is excellent for helping to keep the subject alive and for showing students the type of subject matter which should find its way into their newspaper cuttings book. The author hopes to produce this book annually.

Westminster Workshop (Pergamon Press, 1967). An attractive guide to the constitution to put in the hands of first-year students. 'A' level candidates turn to it at revision time. It is particularly well set out with the points listed and arguments for discussion added.

Jennings, Sir Ivor. *The British Constitution* (O.U.P.). Although first published in 1941 this book is still well worth putting in the hands of 'O' level candidates. An authority introduces them to discussion of issues beyond the mere facts in the textbooks and helps them to destroy the notion that the subject is 'incredibly boring' (see Denis Lawton in *New Society*, 25 April 1968).

White, L. W. and Hussey, W. H. *Government in Great Britain and the Commonwealth*, 4th ed. (C.U.P., 1965). This is a useful textbook for the 'O' level candidate. It deals adequately with the various branches of the constitution, though it devotes a disproportionate amount of space to the Commonwealth.

THE NATURE AND SPIRIT OF THE CONSTITUTION – ITS CONVENTIONS AND TRADITIONS

Amory, L. S. *Thoughts on the Constitution* (O.U.P., 1953). A small provocative book by a politician of immense experience and great learning.

Brasher, N. H. *Studies in British Government* (Macmillan, 1964). A recent look at the constitution at work by a schoolmaster, who is a historian, it is concerned with the steady evolution of the unwritten constitution.

Beer, S. *Modern British Politics* (Faber, 1965). A penetrating inquiry into the attitudes of British politicians by an American who manages to be quite impartial.

Butler, D. E. and Freeman, J. *British Political Facts 1900–1967* (Macmillan, 1967). A most useful collection of information about cabinets, cabinet ministers, statistics of general elections, etc.

Butler, D. E. and King, A. *The British General Election of 1966* (Macmillan, 1966). The latest in a series of studies of recent elections, relating the campaigns as they were fought by the parties and analysing the results.

Rose, R. (ed.) *Studies in British Politics and Policy-Making in Britain* (Macmillan, 1966). These are collections of essays by distinguished students of contemporary British politics, not normally available to the general reader.

Sampson, A. *Anatomy of Britain Today* (Hodder and Stoughton, 1965). A witty discriminating look at our political institutions and the people who participate in animating them, like bankers, trade union leaders, industrialists, bishops, etc. It reminds us of the important fact that politics is concerned with human beings.

172

APPENDIX I

Finer, S. E. *Anonymous Empire* (Pall Mall, 1966). A shrewd study of the pressure groups who are continuously pushing and prodding M.P.'s behind the scenes.

Marshall, G. and Moodie, G. C. *Some Problems of the Constitution* (Hutchinson, 1961). This little book provides useful material for understanding and answering the sort of questions that are set at 'A' level.

Guttsman, W. L. *The British Political Elite* (MacGibbon and Kee, 1963). This is another study by a scholarly American of the background of British politicians, their education, their professions, etc.

Dicey, A. V. *Law and the Constitution* (Papermac). A nineteenth-century classic well worth putting in the library. Even if the 'A' level candidates read only two or three chapters, they will have met Dicey (whom they should know) and his lucid style with difficult ideas cannot but do them good.

Wade and Phillips. *Constitutional Law* (Longmans, 1965). Another useful reference book for the library. This is where they can find out, for example, just what statutory regulations are.

Wiseman, H. V. *Parliament and the Executive* (Routledge and Paul, 1966). This book brings together within one volume important writings of a hundred authorities. A very useful book for illustrating the diversity of views that can be held on political institutions and for introducing the student to writers he should know about.

THE CABINET

Jennings, Sir Ivor. *Cabinet Government* (C.U.P., 1959). A monumental study complete with chapter and verse that will need to be revised by some other hand if it is not to become out of date. The essential principles are, however, in it and are not likely to change.

Carter, C. B. *The Office of Prime Minister* (Faber, 1956). A scholarly and painstaking study by an American professor.

Benemy, F. W. G. *The Elected Monarch* (Harrap, 1964). An argument that the power of the Prime Minister has recently grown enormously.

Mackintosh, J. P. *The British Cabinet* (Stevens, 1968). A long, carefully documented, very readable book by a professor who is now an M.P.; and which, in its latest edition, is refreshed by much up-to-date personal acquaintance with ministers and their mysterious ways.

Daalder, H. *Cabinet Reform in Britain 1914–1963* (O.U.P., 1967). A Dutch professor examines in great detail the evolution of the British cabinet system.

Butt, R. *The Powers of Parliament* (Constable, 1968). A distinguished political journalist discusses trenchantly and authoritatively the relationships between the government, the opposition and back benchers, in the quest for and exercise of political power. This is an up-to-date (1968) view.

THE HOUSE OF COMMONS

Chester, D. N. and Bowring, N. *Questions in Parliament* (O.U.P., 1962). This brings out the kind of questions asked by M.P.s in order to keep a check on ministers.

Hanson, A. H. and Wiseman, H. V. *Parliament at Work* (Stevens, 1962). Two experienced university teachers join in illustrating the work of the Commons by selected examples from debates.

173

TEACHING OF ECONOMICS IN SECONDARY SCHOOLS

Taylor, Dr Eric. *The House of Commons at Work* (Penguin Books). A Clerk of the House describes the procedure by which the Commons carries out its functions.

Jennings, Sir Ivor. *Parliament* (C.U.P., 1961). A compendious tome with a wealth of example and some legal wit, almost a definitive work on the subject.

The Queen's Government (Penguin Books, 1960). In lighter vein, written for the man-in-the-street, but very well worth reading, nevertheless.

Morrison, Lord. *Government and Parliament* (O.U.P., 1964). An admirable account by a most experienced parliamentarian of the constitution at work. A minister of long standing the author is eminently practical and well informed.

Laundy, P. *The Office of the Speaker* (Cassell, 1964). A thorough examination and a full historical account of the development of this most important Member of Parliament.

Richards, P. G. *Honourable Members* (Faber, 1959). This is a study of back benchers and their efforts to keep the government under the control of Parliament.

Crick, B. *The Reform of Parliament* (Weidenfeld and Nicholson, 1964). A most penetrating and up-to-date analysis of the weaknesses of the House of Commons and how they might be remedied by an eminent university teacher who is passionately concerned with parliamentary government.

Campion, Lord (ed.). *Parliament – A Survey* (Allen and Unwin, 1963). Different aspects of Parliament seen by a dozen different authorities. This is a valuable book for second year students who already know the basic facts and are ready to be made to realise that there are different points of view.

King, H. *Parliament and Freedom* (John Murray, 1966). An attractive little book for the library. It gives the historical background of much of what happens in Parliament and has the cachet of being written by Mr Speaker.

The Times. The House of Commons (1966). An accurate analysis of the results of the general election of 1966 and a biography of each candidate. This is one of a series of similar reference books produced by *The Times* with characteristic thoroughness and imposing weightiness.

THE PARTY SYSTEM

Mackenzie, R. T. *British Political Parties* (Heinemann, 1967). A compendious account of how the parties work today by a professor. The latest edition contains a chapter on recent events.

Jennings, Sir Ivor. *Party Politics*, 3 vols. (C.U.P., 1962). Clearly from the same stable as *Cabinet Government* and *Parliament*, the author goes into the matter with great gusto, uses some of Laski's methods of analysis. A teacher's book, probably.

Bulmer-Thomas, Ivor. *The Growth of the British Party System* (John Baker, 1965). A very well informed and readable history of the British parties by a sound scholar who did not find Parliament much to his liking and is indeed a victim of party politics.

THE CROWN

Nicholson, Sir Harold. *King George V* (Constable, 1952).

Wheeler Bennett, Sir John. *King George VI* (Macmillan, 1958). These two biographies, based on the official papers, are a superb insight into the powers and influence of a modern British monarch.

Benemy, F. W. G. *The Queen Reigns* (Harrap, 1963). This is a short study of the powers of the Queen today, which contains many examples of the Queen at work that the student should find useful.

Martin, Kingsley. *The Crown and the Establishment* (Hutchinson, 1962, in cloth; Penguin Books, 1967).

Petrie, Sir Charles. *The Modern British Monarchy* (Eyre and Spottiswoode, 1962). These two books should be read in conjunction because Kingsley Martin is a relatively hostile critic and Petrie is almost fulsome in his admiration.

Fulford, R. *Hanover to Windsor* (Batsford, 1960).

Kenyon, J. P. *The Stuarts* (Batsford, 1958).

Morris, C. *The Tudors* (Batsford, 1955).

Plumb, J. H. *The First Four Georges* (Batsford, 1956). These four books are in a series and given an excellent historical account of the Crown. They are available as paperbacks.

BIOGRAPHIES

Avon, Lord. *Full Circle* (Cassell).

Blake, Robert. *Disraeli* (Eyre and Spottiswoode).

The Unknown Prime Minister, Bonar Law (Eyre and Spottiswoode).

Birkenhead, Lord. *The Life of Lord Halifax* (Hamish Hamilton).

Jenkins, Roy. *Asquith* (Collins).

Macmillan, Harold. *Autobiography*. 3 vols. (Macmillan).

Nicolson, Nigel (ed.). *The Diaries of Harold Nicolson* (Collins).

Owen, Frank. *Tempestuous Journey (A Life of Lloyd George)* (Cassell).

Young, Kenneth. *A. J. Balfour* (Bell).

THE CIVIL SERVICE

Campbell, G. A. *The Civil Service in Britain* (Penguin Books, 1955). A readable account of the work of the Civil Service which contains a great deal of detail that the student will probably find unnecessary to know.

The New Whitehall (Series published by Allen and Unwin). Each book is written by a former head of a government department who therefore writes with great authority and knowledge of his subject. The most useful books are perhaps those on *The Foreign Office, The Colonial Office, The Home Office,* and *The Treasury.* The organisation and functions of each department are admirably set out and discussed.

Chester, D. N. (ed.). *The Organisation of British Central Government* (Allen and Unwin). This is a compendious account of the way in which Whitehall works given by a working party appointed by the Royal Institute of Public Administration.

The Reports of the Fulton Committee (H.M.S.O.) give a very full description of the Service, its history, its weaknesses, and how it should be reformed.

THE LAW IN BRITAIN

Wade, E. C. S. *Constitutional Law* (Longman, 1967). An immense review of the whole constitution by an eminent teacher of law. This book could almost be used as a basic textbook.

Yardley, D. C. M. *Introduction to British Constitutional Law* (Butterworth, 1969). In terse style this little book examines the British idea of the rule of law, the common law, the organisation of the courts, the fundamental statutes like the Act of Settlement.

Archer, P. *The Queen's Courts* (Penguin Books, 1956). A popular description of the English courts.

Jackson, R. M. *The Machinery of Justice in England*, 5th ed. (C.U.P., 1967). This is probably the fullest, most authoritative discussion of the English judiciary, their functions and background there is, but it is a book for the teacher rather than the taught.

Hanbury, H. G. *English Courts of Law* (O.U.P., 1960). A shorter version of the book by Jackson.

Henston, R. F. V. *Lives of the Lord Chancellors 1885–1940* (O.U.P.). An excellent picture of the kind of lawyer who attains this characteristically English office in which all the political powers meet.

ENGLISH LOCAL GOVERNMENT

Local Government in Britain (H.M.S.O.). A Central Office of Information pamphlet which contains in concise form the heart of the matter.

Jackson, R. M. *The Machinery of Local Government* (Macmillan, 1965). This is a scholarly, legalistic account of local government by a legal academic who has had considerable personal experience of the subject.

Jackson, W. E. *The Structure of Local Government in England and Wales* (Penguin Books, 1959). A popular account.

Warren, J. H. *The English Local Government System*, revised by P. G. Richards (Allen and Unwin, 1965). This is a factual, accurate, description of what happens.

Cole, Margaret. *Servant of the County* (Dobson, 1956). The author looks back nostalgically on a long career in the cause of the London County Council.

Benham, H. *Two Cheers for the Town Hall* (Hutchinson, 1964). A journalist with personal experience of being a councillor gives a cheerful and witty account of his adventures and misadventures, including some shrewd criticism.

Headrick, T. E. *The Town Clerk in English Local Government* (Allen and Unwin, 1962). A scholarly examination of the work of this local government officer.

Report of the Maud Committee on Management of Local Government (H.M.S.O., 1967). The report is too detailed for most sixth formers, but its recommendations are worth reading.

THE COMMONWEALTH

Wiseman, H. V. *Britain and The Commonwealth* (Allen and Unwin, 1967). An up-to-date analysis of the relationship between the United Kingdom and her former colonies.

Miller, J. D. B. *The Commonwealth in the World* (Duckworth, 1965). An Australian professor considers the political relations of the Commonwealth with the rest of the world.

Henssler, R. *Yesterday's Rulers* (O.U.P.). An American examines the British Colonial Civil Service.

Morris, J. *Pax Britanica* (Faber, 1968). A brilliant account of the climax of the British Empire.

APPENDIX I

The Making of a Nation. Pamphlets by the Central Office of Information (H.M.S.O.). The following are still in print: *Sierra Leone, Jamaica, Uganda, Kenya, Malta, Guyana.*

The Commonwealth Office Year Book 1968 (H.M.S.O.) is a mine of useful information.

The *Corona* books (H.M.S.O.) are well illustrated, admirably written accounts of former British colonies and their development. They give particularly interesting pictures of the people concerned, their way of life, the relationship with the British, etc.

JOURNALS

The weeklies such as *The Spectator, The New Statesman, The Economist, The Listener* and *New Society* from time to time contain most helpful articles. You will have to keep your eyes open and recommend reading to the students.

The best national newspapers, the so-called 'quality press', are worth reading and furnish material for scrapbooks. *The Times, The Daily Telegraph, The Guardian, The Sunday Times* and *The Observer* between them give a vivid account of the news.

There are four quarterly journals which should be taken. They are:

Parliamentary Affairs, published by the Hansard Society for Parliamentary Government, 162 Buckingham Palace Road, London S.W.1. You can join as an individual or the school can join.

Public Administration, the journal of the Royal Institute of Public Administration, 24 Park Crescent, London W.1.

The Political Quarterly, 49 Park Lane, London W.1.

The Round Table, 18 Northumberland Avenue, London W.C.2., a commonwealth quarterly.

APPENDIX II

Printed source material

There is a constant stream of literature on all aspects of the subject of Economics poured out by the government and by the public relations offices of many firms both in industry and commerce. Most of this literature is obtainable free of charge and frequently in sufficient quantities to provide copies for each of your pupils. Many of these institutions also provide wall charts and other visual aids, free of charge. The titles of some of the better known publications, together with an indication of where they can be obtained, are listed below.

OFFICIAL GOVERNMENT-SPONSORED PUBLICATIONS

D.E.A. Progress Reports. Published monthly by the Department of Economic Affairs and obtainable from Publications Division (H), Central Office of Information, Hercules Road, London S.E.1.

Broadsheets on Britain. Published monthly by, and obtainable from, the Central Office of Information.

E.F.T.A. Bulletin. Published by, and obtainable from, the European Free Trade Association Information Centre, 1 Victoria Street, London S.W.1. Occasional booklets dealing with specific E.F.T.A. matters are also obtainable, free of charge.

Fact Sheets on Britain. A series of pamphlets and booklets published by the Central Office of Information. A list is obtainable from H.M.S.O., P.O. Box 569, Hercules Road, London S.E.1.

Digest of Statistics. Monthly from H.M.S.O.

National Income and Expenditure. Annually from H.M.S.O.

Balance of Payments. Periodically from H.M.S.O.

Bank of England. Quarterly bulletin.

Britain in Figures. A plastic wallet card containing statistical information about the economy. Published by the C.O.I. for the Board of Trade and available from Board of Trade Headquarters and regional offices.

BANK REVIEWS

The large commercial banks publish quarterly reviews containing articles written by distinguished contributors. They are published free of charge and may be obtained from the addresses given below. Most of them can be sent direct to your school from your local branch bank. The banks also publish wall-charts and information sheets on various topics.

Barclay's Bank Review. Barclay's Bank Economic Intelligence Department, 54 Lombard Street, London E.C.3. This review includes a useful series of charts and statistics showing recent economic trends.

Lloyds' Bank Review. 71 Lombard Street, London E.C.3. Copies can also be obtained from branch banks.

Midland Bank Review. The Manager, Economics Department, Midland Bank Ltd, Poultry, London, E.C.2.

APPENDIX II

Three Banks Review. Glyn, Mills and Co., 67 Lombard Street, London E.C.3; William Deacons Bank Ltd., Mosley Street, Manchester; Royal Bank of Scotland, St Andrew Square, Edinburgh 2.

The National, Westminster Bank Review. An amalgamation of the Westminster, National Provincial and District Bank Reviews. Obtainable from 41 Lothbury, London E.C.2.

MISCELLANEOUS

About Credit. Published by the Consumers' Council on the numerous ways in which a consumer can borrow money. Issued free to schools.

The British Economy in Figures. A very detailed and useful folder published by Lloyds Bank Ltd; obtainable from the Public Relations Officer, Lloyds Bank Ltd, P.O. Box 215, 71 Lombard Street, London E.C.3.

British Steel. Quarterly, published by the British Steel Corporation, 22 Kingsway, London W.C.2.

Conjoncture. A well informed broadsheet published monthly by the French bank, Société Génerale. Obtainable free from the London office at 105 Broad Street, London E.C.2.

The Economist. Weekly. Special rates offered to students.

Esso Petroleum Co. Ltd publishes booklets such as *The Economic Facts of Life, The Way to Understanding* and *Local Government.* Obtainable from Public Relations Department, Victoria Street, London S.W.1.

Hill, Samuel and Co. Ltd, 100 Wood Street, E.C.2, publish occasional papers on monetary and banking matters.

The Hobart Papers. Published by the Institute of Economic Affairs, 7 Hobart Place, London S.W.1. A series of pamphlets on particular topics such as taxation.

Institute of Bankers. Quarterly journal from the Institute of Bankers, Lombard Street, London E.C.3.

Money and the Citizen. A series of booklets on different aspects of money, published by the National Savings Committee, free of charge.

The New Scientist. Weekly. Special rates are obtainable for students.

Political and Economic Planning (PEP). 16 Queen Anne's Gate, London S.W.1, publish regular papers on specialised topics.

Progress. Published free by Unilever, Unilever House, Blackfriars, London E.C.4. Unilever also publish reprints of speeches and lectures in booklet form on such topics as 'Capital Investment'.

Profit and Loss. A highly entertaining game which teaches the principles of bookkeeping and business economics. Available from S. Pritchard, P.O. Box 2, Grantham, Lincs.

Visual material

THE EDUCATIONAL FOUNDATION FOR VISUAL AIDS

Little can be said about visual material and methods of teaching before mention is made of this invaluable organisation. It produces catalogues, by subjects, of visual material including wall charts, filmstrips and films, currently available. Most of the film material listed can be hired from the Foundation Film Library, Brooklands House, Weybridge, Surrey, and filmstrips are available for inspection by teachers. It provides, through the National Committee for Visual Aids in

179

Education, an information service about the various methods of projecting audio-visual and visual material, providing, for instance, reports on the performance and value of video-tape recorders currently on the market, and publishes the periodical *Visual Education* monthly. The address is 33 Queen Anne Street, London, S.W.1.

CLASSROOM MATERIAL

The Bank Education Service, 10 Lombard Street, London E.C.3, publishes useful, clear and attractive wall charts with accompanying booklets, on all aspects of banking. It also provides trained lecturers who will visit the school to speak on banking topics free of charge. A 'Banking Kit' of cheques and forms for use in the classroom is also available.

Educational Productions Ltd, East Ardsley, Wakefield, Yorks., produce wall charts to illustrate the 'Structure of Industry' and the 'Pattern of Trade'.

The Pictorial Charts Unit, 153 Uxbridge Road, London W.7, produces visual material on 'The Bank of England', 'Simple Economics' and 'National Problems'.

The Stock Exchange. Two wall charts on the operation of the stock market are obtainable, together with explanatory notes, from The Public Relations Officer, The Stock Exchange, London, E.C.2.

35-mm FILMSTRIPS

Very few filmstrips are as yet available to the Economics teacher. A selection of those that are available is listed:

Common Ground. Obtainable from the Educational Supply Association Ltd, Pinnacles, Harlow, Essex. Those on Economics include, *Why Have Money?* and *An Introduction to Economics*.

McGraw-Hill Publishing Co. Ltd, Film Department, Shoppenhangers Road, Maidenhead, Berks., have a series on *Samuelson's Economics*.

Pitmans publish *The Family Budget* and *The National Budget*.

Encyclopaedia Britannica publish *Basic Economics*.

16-mm FILM LIBRARIES

There are very many 16-mm film libraries, a good proportion of which specialise in 'sponsored' or documentary films. Those libraries containing films of use and interest to the Economics class are listed below. Some of them have a number of films which you may wish to use, others have only one or two. The only approach is to obtain the catalogues of the various libraries and to make your own choice from the often detailed description of the films to be found in the catalogues. The catalogues obtainable from the following libraries will probably be the most useful:

British Film Institute, 42/43 Lower Marsh, London S.E.1 (also the Education Department of the Institute at 20 Old Compton Street, London W.1).

British Iron and Steel Federation, Film Library, Wilton Crescent, London S.W.19.

British Transport Films, Melbury House, Melbury Terrace, London N.W.1.

Central Film Library, Government Buildings, Bromyard Avenue, Acton, W.3.

Concord Films Council, Nacton, Ipswich, Suffolk.

E.F.V.A. Foundation Film Library, Brooklands House, Weybridge, Surrey.

APPENDIX II

Educational and Television Films, 2 Doughty Street, London W.C.1.

Esso Film Library, Public Relations Department, Esso Petroleum Co. Ltd., Victoria Street, London S.W.1.

Ford Film Library, 25 The Burroughs, Hendon, London N.W.4.

Gas Council Film Library, 6/7 Great Chapel Street, London W.1.

I.C.I. Film Library, Imperial Chemical House, Millbank, London S.W.1.

National Coal Board Film Library, 26/28 Dorset Square, London N.W.1.

Petroleum Films Bureau, 4 Brook Street, Hanover Square, London W.1.

Rank Sponsored Film Library, P.O. Box 70, Great West Road, Brentford, Middlesex.

Shell-Mex Film Library, 25 The Burroughs, Hendon, London N.W.4.

Sound Services Ltd, Wilton Crescent, Merton Park, London S.W.19.

Unilever Film Library, Unilever House, Blackfriars, London E.C.4.